D1645068

CHURCHILL: THE WAR LEADER, 1940-1945

Churchill's road to destiny

In March 1916 Winston Churchill was serving as a lieutenant-colonel on the Western Front when he narrowly missed being killed by a German shell. '20 yards more to the left', he wrote to his wife, Clementine, and it would have been 'a good ending to a chequered life, a final gift - unvalued - to an ungrateful country - an impoverishment of the war-making power of Britain which no one would ever know or measure or mourn'.[1]

Over thirty years later, Churchill recalled the events of May 1940 in his memoirs. Commenting on the fulfilment of his lifelong wish to assume the highest political office in his country, he said: 'At last I had the authority to give directions over the whole scene. I felt as if I were walking with destiny, and that all my past life had been but a preparation for this hour and for this trial.'[2] Although Churchill had long aspired to the premiership, his appointment on 10 May 1940 did not have about it the air of inevitability that decades of distance from the war and the afterglow of his achievements have bestowed upon it.

Throughout his long parliamentary career, which had begun in 1900 and had seen him passing through almost every major office of state, Churchill had been frequently reviled by his fellow MPs. In August 1939 Duff Cooper, a former First Lord of the Admiralty, anticipated the political crisis of the following year, and captured the contemporary dichotomy of views on Churchill: 'What are the alternatives? - Halifax or Winston. I don't really believe the former is up to it, and the latter has so many and such violent enemies - not only in the House, but there are large numbers of people in the country who admire but don't trust him.'[3]

On Great Britain's entry into the war on 3 September 1939, Churchill was appointed to the Cabinet and to the Admiralty as First Lord - a post which he 'had quitted in pain and sorrow almost exactly a quarter of a century before',[4] after the failure of the Dardanelles expedition in the First World War. The move was seen as a mark of the government's progression from appeasement to a firm commitment to the fight.

With his long working day and his constant flow of notes and calls to every department involved in the war, Churchill rapidly reinforced his personal and complete commitment to the task and his keenness to play as full a part as possible. In October 1939 Prime Minister Neville Chamberlain appointed him to the Military Co-ordination Committee ('a body for pre-digestion of Defence topics',[5] as the Secretary to the Cabinet, Sir Edward Bridges, described it), which Churchill came to dominate and, from April 1940, to chair. The Committee had responsibility for the actions of the principal ministries involved in the conduct of the war, but, not being chaired by the Prime Minister, it lacked any real power. The experience greatly influenced Churchill's own organization of government and the prosecution of the war when he assumed office.

The Committee's lack of purpose was especially demonstrated in its failure to co-ordinate the conduct of the operations in Norway which finally began on 8 April 1940, after months of prevarication and fruitless debate with the French Allies. This, the first major British military engagement of the war, aimed at forestalling a German invasion of Norway, was a costly and abject failure, for which Churchill himself had to accept some of the blame.

Shortly after Parliament had spent two days debating and haranguing Chamberlain for the failure of the Norway expedition, the German invasion of Belgium and Holland on 10 May 1940 brought the crisis to a head. Away from the debate, pressure groups were forming which narrowed the candidates for Chamberlain's successor down to two men: Churchill and the Foreign Secretary, Lord Halifax (**document 2**).

1

The diaries of the then Chief of the Imperial General Staff, General Sir Edmund Ironside, reflected a widely held view about Churchill: 'Naturally the only man who can succeed is Winston and he is too unstable, though he has the genius to bring the war to an end.'[6] Halifax was Chamberlain's choice. He enjoyed much support in Parliament and, as was later revealed, he would also have been the King's first choice.[7]

It was only after Halifax refused the premiership that Churchill, according to his own account of the proceedings, quietly and humbly accepted. One of his principal supporters, Leo Amery MP, commented: 'Churchill, the one man by common consent ruled out from ever becoming the Prime Minister of any party, was, by equally common consent, welcomed as the only possible leader in the hour of danger.'[8]

Churchill's finest hour

Churchill came to power at a time when Great Britain faced one of the greatest challenges in its history. In May 1940 Germany, having occupied Czechoslovakia and Poland, and overrun large parts of Scandinavia, was in the process of invading Belgium and Holland and was beginning offensive action against France. While Churchill held to a belief in the power and efficiency of the French Army and publicly expressed supreme confidence in his country's will and ability to resist, the views that he put forward in private were sometimes rather less sanguine. As he returned from Buckingham Palace after his formal appointment by the King as Prime Minister, his personal detective, Inspector Thompson, highlighted the scope of the task that lay ahead. 'God alone knows how great it is', Churchill replied. 'All I hope is that it is not too late. I am very much afraid it is.'[9]

As the Germans relentlessly advanced in France, Churchill adamantly opposed suggestions in Cabinet that negotiations for 'decent terms' might be opened with Hitler, and brought the majority of his ministers round to his view. He resisted French demands (and loud murmuring among British forces on the ground) for more air cover, preferring to follow the advice of his Commander-in-Chief, Fighter Command, Air Chief Marshal Sir Hugh Dowding, and kept back resources for the anticipated forthcoming aerial onslaught on the United Kingdom.

By the end of May 1940 the British and French forces had been pushed back against the sea at Dunkirk, with nowhere to turn. The British press saw parallels with the position of Field Marshal Haig's forces on the Western Front in March 1918, facing the sudden German offensive, but holding firm, with their 'backs to the walls' (**document 1**).

Churchill's personal Chief of Staff, General Sir Hastings Ismay, records that, shortly before Dunkirk, the Chiefs of Staff concluded that 'Germany has most of the cards; but the real test is whether the morale of our fighting personnel and civil population will counter-balance the numerical and material advantages which Germany enjoys. We believe it will.'[10] Churchill's view was simple:

> our prestige in Europe was very low. The only way we could get it back was by showing the world that Germany had not beaten us. If, after two or three months, we could show that we were still unbeaten, our prestige would return. Even if we were beaten, we should be no worse off than we should be if we were now to abandon the struggle. Let us therefore avoid being dragged down the slippery slope with France.[11]

It was in this context that Churchill's true genius showed itself, effectively making him the iconic figure that he has remained ever since. Through a series of speeches and personal rallying calls to the country, he managed to exploit the 'miracle' of Dunkirk and, while making clear that 'wars are not won by evacuations', crucially prevented the nation from sinking into the defeatism that had overtaken its French ally. Through the power and skill of his oratory in broadcasts to Britain (**document 3**), he raised and sustained the national morale, at a time when it was to form the

2

backbone of the country's resistance. Despite the desperate defensive position of the Battle of Britain and the devastation, carnage and suffering caused by the Blitz, the British people shared their Prime Minister's emotional argument that defied any contrary rationale, and agreed that they would 'never surrender'. In German-occupied territories too his stirring broadcasts brought a spark of hope and 'his voice', as General Ismay found in post-war visits to Scandinavia, 'was the only ray of light in an otherwise completely dark and hopeless world'.[12]

Churchill, Roosevelt and the US Alliance

Details of the Dunkirk evacuations were broadcast widely in the USA and, like the constant stories of heroism in the Battle of Britain and hardships endured in the Blitz that followed, had a profound effect on American public opinion and admiration for the British people. However, opinion polls at the time continued to show that a majority of Americans opposed direct participation in the war.

The war was being fought over British territory with meagre British resources, backed only by forces from the Dominions and a small number of foreign nationals who had avoided German capture. That resistance to Hitler was absolutely necessary was a solid tenet of Churchill's philosophy. He was equally clear, however, that, while Britain must hold out, ultimate victory could not be achieved without American aid.

In his speech of 4 June 1940 he thundered out a message aimed not only at British listeners, but also at the American audience that regularly heard his broadcasts relayed on US radio:

> we shall not flag or fail. We shall go on to the end . . . we shall defend our island, whatever the cost may be . . . we shall never surrender, and even if, which I do not for a moment believe, this island or a large part of it were subjugated and starving, then our Empire beyond the seas, armed and guarded by the British fleet, would carry on the struggle, until, in God's good time, the new world, with all its power and might, steps forth to the rescue and the liberation of the old.[13]

A fortnight later, on 18 June, the day of France's collapse, he highlighted even more starkly the global scale of the threat that Hitler represented: 'If we can stand up to him, all Europe may be free . . . But if we fail, then the whole world, including the United States . . . will sink into the abyss of a new Dark Age.'[14]

Churchill had recognized, long before the outbreak of the Second World War, that American involvement in any conflict with Germany would be vital, if victory were to be achieved, and he had made this view plain on his pre-war visits to the USA. However, he was fighting against a general reluctance on the part of the American people to become directly involved in the war and his repeated arguments failed to alter this.

On 15 June 1940 Churchill had sent a telegram to President Roosevelt supporting the French Prime Minister's request for an expression of American support. In it he repeated a plea that he had made a month previously for 'forty or fifty of your older destroyers' to assist in the Battle of the Atlantic, in which, by the end of that year, Britain was suffering average monthly shipping losses of 400,000 tons. However, by late 1940, although the American public were offering every sympathy and personal aid to a British people sorely pressed by enemy air raids, they still remained unwilling to become active participants in the war with Germany.

The American administration had doubts about Britain's ability to resist a German invasion. Churchill's telegram to Roosevelt on 15 June 1940 countered this argument by highlighting the risks to the USA that the fall of Great Britain and its becoming a 'vassal state of the Hitler Empire'[15] would represent. The same message, however, assured the President on one of his principal concerns, namely that, if Britain fell, it would 'never fail to send the Fleet across the Atlantic'.[16] A graphic illustration of Churchill's determination to stop valuable war material falling to the Germans was provided on 3 July 1940 when he sanctioned the attack on the French fleet sheltering in the port of Mers-el-Kébir in Algeria.

On 13 August Roosevelt sent his most favourable response yet to Churchill, offering to supply the requested destroyers, but demanding in return 99-year leases to bases in the West Indies, Newfoundland and Bermuda.

With the presidential victory of 5 November behind him, Roosevelt's policy began to show signs of a shift. He agreed with his Cabinet's proposal in mid-November to open Anglo-American staff talks and approved his military planners' secret contingency proposals in the event of an Axis attack on the United States, whereby supplies to Great Britain would be maintained.

Britain needed extensive military supplies and, as Churchill knew, the only country with the capacity to produce these was the United States. However, the American administration was demanding large advances before agreeing to commit its resources, not least, as the British Ambassador to the USA, Lord Lothian, reported to Churchill, because the Americans suspected the British of having 'vast resources available that we have not yet disclosed'.[17] In his letter of 8 December 1940 to the President, Churchill painted a bleak prospect for the military situation across the globe in 1941, if more American support were not forthcoming, adding that 'The moment approaches when we shall no longer be able to pay cash for shipping and other supplies.'[18] In emotional, but brutal terms, he emphasized that it would be of advantage to nobody 'if at the height of this struggle Great Britain were to be divested of all saleable assets, so that after the victory was won with our blood, civilisation saved, and the time gained for the United States to be fully armed against all eventualities, we should stand stripped to the bone'.[19] He added the simple economic argument that such behaviour then would entail Britain being unable, after the war, to afford to buy American imports, resulting in widespread unemployment in the United States.

Roosevelt's considered 'reply' came in the form of a press conference on 17 December in which he described his solution to the problem of 'the dollar sign'. His plan, which was couched in terms of American self-interest and minimizing the economic risk, came to be known as 'Lend-Lease'. Under it the United States would supply military material in return for some short-term payments in the form of assets in the USA and gold reserves, but largely by means of payments deferred until after the end of the war. He sent a strong message of support, quoting Longfellow (**document 4**), which prompted Churchill's equally famous response, in his broadcast of 9 February 1941: 'Give us the tools, and we will finish the job.'[20] The Lend-Lease Act became law on 11 March 1941.

Churchill was in regular telegraphic contact with the US President and was beginning to establish a warm relationship, although against a background of American caution and mutual cynicism. The close friendship between the two leaders was, however, more firmly established by their first meeting, which took place on board the US cruiser *Augusta* and the battle-cruiser HMS *Prince of Wales*, in Placentia Bay, Newfoundland between 9 and 12 August 1941.

The meeting produced a significant declaration of common principles which came to be known as the 'Atlantic Charter', but which was kept secret until simultaneously announced on both sides of the Atlantic on 14 August (**document 5**). Despite disagreements and individual reinterpretations of aspects of the wording, the Charter was also accepted by the Soviet Union and was to form the basis for the declaration of the United Nations at the end of 1941.

Although Churchill's high hopes of a greater commitment from Roosevelt, following the Atlantic Conference, did not immediately materialize, subsequent offensive actions by U-boats against American naval vessels in the Atlantic in September and October led to an increasing drift away from the policy of neutrality. The policy was finally abandoned after the Japanese attack on Pearl Harbour on 7 December, which led to the declaration by Britain and the United States of war against Japan, and Germany's subsequent declaration of war against the United States. Churchill was entirely confident that American participation in the war 'with time and patience will give certain victory'.[21] In his letter to the King, Roosevelt sealed the Alliance with the words: 'Our two nations are now full comrades-in-arms.'[22]

Churchill and his generals

Churchill, unlike Roosevelt, was not a head of state, and his responsibilities did not, therefore, include those of Commander-in-Chief of the Armed Forces. However, on taking office as Prime Minister in May 1940, Churchill assumed the role of Minister of Defence, though emphasizing to Parliament that his responsibility for overseeing military operations was shared with the professional heads of the armed services, the Chiefs of Staff. The war, he said, was

> conducted from day to day, and in its future outlook, by the Chiefs of Staff Committee . . . They give executive directions and orders to the Commanders-in-Chief in the various theatres . . . I do not think there has ever been a system in which professional heads of the fighting Services have had a freer hand . . . or have received more constant and harmonious support from the Prime Minister and the Cabinet under whom they serve.[23]

Later, in his memoirs, Churchill summed up his attitude: 'It is easier to give directions than advice, and more agreeable to have the right to act, even in a limited sphere, than the privilege to talk at large.'[24] The assumption of power as Prime Minister was, for him, not merely the fulfilment of ambition, but the opportunity to put his ideas into practice.

Churchill's capacity as a strategist, however, is something about which even his closest staff held doubts. Sir Ian Jacob, Assistant Secretary to the Cabinet for most of the war and one of Churchill's most loyal supporters, wrote in 1968 that 'One is bound to question whether Churchill could be classed as a strategist at all.' In his view, Churchill did not 'weigh up carefully the resources available . . . the possible courses of action open to the enemy, and then, husbanding and concentrating his forces, strike at the selected spot'.[25] In General Sir Archibald Wavell's view, 'Winston's tactical ideas had to some extent crystallised at the South African War',[26] or, as Jacob put it, he 'tended to think that, even in the modern age, determined men with rifles and bayonets were all that was wanted to withstand attack'.[27] This was borne out by Churchill's signal to Wavell of 7 January 1941 in which he lamented the 'disproportionately small' ratio of his fighting strength to the number of support services. Churchill's scheme of things demanded, in Jacob's words, 'constant action on as wide a scale as possible; the enemy must be made continually to "bleed and burn" '.[28] It was his 'impetuous nature, his gambler's spirit, and his determination to follow his own selected path at all costs'[29] that added to the reservations of the future Chief of the Imperial General Staff, Alan Brooke, when he was offered the post in November 1941.

Despite any personal concerns expressed in the intimacy of his diaries, Brooke remained one of Churchill's most fervent admirers. Major-General Sir John Kennedy, his Director of Military Operations, reflecting on Churchill in his memoir of 1957, also makes clear that the Chiefs of Staff were 'agreed that his great qualities made up for the vast amount of work, often useless as we thought, which he imposed upon the staffs'.[30] General Ismay likened Churchill to Alexander the Great, and claimed that 'a nation which is so fortunate as to produce a Churchill at the critical moment would surely be insane if it did not give the fullest rein to his unrivalled experience and qualifications', adding in his support that 'Not once during the whole war did he overrule his military advisers on a purely military question.'[31]

Ismay also notes that the Prime Minister exercised 'personal, direct, ubiquitous and continuous supervision, not only over the formulation of military policy at every stage, but also over the general conduct of military operations',[32] and it was this aspect of Churchill's approach which was to become a source of irritation to many of his generals in the field. Nowhere is this better illustrated than in his copious communications with his two successive Commanders-in-Chief, Middle East, General Sir Archibald Wavell and General Claude Auchinleck.

The rather scholarly and taciturn character of Wavell conflicted sharply with the more emotional and impromptu personality of Churchill, and the relationship was never an easy one. Churchill was often exasperated by Wavell's complaints about the minimal or poor resources of material and manpower with which he had to fight on an ever increasing number of fronts, and by his insistence on careful preparations before undertaking any major military operation, which Churchill interpreted as excessively cautious. To urge him on, Churchill sent Wavell a stream of telegrams containing detailed observations on potential operations. In one particularly long example on 23 August 1940 he gave Wavell meticulous instructions for the deployment of his forces, large parts of which Wavell simply disregarded.

In Churchill's eyes Wavell failed to exploit the opportunity offered by the reinforcement of his tank force by the quickest but most dangerous route, through the Mediterranean, in May 1941. He yet again urged Wavell to 'go on day after day facing all necessary losses until you have beaten the life out of General Rommel's army'.[33] After the failure of the much delayed June 1941 offensive, Wavell was finally relieved of his command and replaced by General Auchinleck, whose preparedness to send troops to quell the revolt in Iraq in April 1941 had so impressed Churchill.

However, in Auchinleck Churchill was faced with a commander who equalled his predecessor's dogged adherence to his own assessment of the military situation in the face of relentless pressure from Churchill and from his Chiefs of Staff. The great, but short-lived success of Auchinleck's first major operation, 'Crusader', in November 1941 brought equally fleeting approbation, as German counter-attacks regained some of the lost ground. There followed the inevitable Churchillian pressure to return to the offensive, particularly at a time when the Russian front looked bleak and Britain was suddenly faced with a new war with the Japanese, who had landed in force on the Malaya Peninsula (**document 6**) and were rapidly to overrun Hong Kong, Singapore and the Netherlands East Indies.

In March 1942 the only prospect for a victory was in north Africa, and Churchill pressed his Chiefs of Staff and commanders vigorously to achieve one. He was incensed by Auchinleck's refusal to come to London for discussions about the situation in north Africa and by his reluctance to be pushed prematurely into an attack for which he felt he lacked the resources. In May 1942 Auchinleck signally failed to stop a German offensive which pushed his armies dangerously far back into Egypt, and the failure of his counter-attack at the end of July sealed his fate. In August Churchill's patience ran out and Auchinleck was replaced as Commander-in-Chief, Middle East by General Harold Alexander, and as Commander of Eighth Army by Lieutenant-General B L Montgomery (**document 7**).

Victory finally came with the success of the Battle of El Alamein in November 1942, which Churchill proudly boasted might at last signal the 'end of the beginning', if not actually the 'beginning of the end'.

Churchill and 'Ultra'

Professor F H Hinsley's voluminous official history *British Intelligence in the Second World War* fully recognizes the value to the Allies of 'Ultra', the data originating from the Government Code and Cipher School (GCCS) at Bletchley Park, which cracked the German Enigma codes.

In particular, Hinsley claims that 'the British forces in north Africa were supplied with more information about more aspects of the enemy's operations than any forces enjoyed during an important campaign of the Second World War', though he adds that 'it did not help the Eighth Army to avoid the reverses . . . that followed when Rommel had halted the British attack of 5-6 June'.[34]

Throughout his political career Churchill had given enormous value to intelligence as a means of gaining advantage against an enemy or potential enemy. In 1924 he wrote: 'I attach more importance to them [decrypts] as a means of forming a true judgement of public policy . . . than to any other sources of knowledge at the disposal of the state.'[35] The product of the first successes of GCCS in cracking the German Enigma codes began to be passed to him shortly after he became Prime Minister in May 1940 and he took a keen, almost obsessive, interest in personally evaluating the data. To protect the security of this uniquely valuable source, circulation of these Ultra decrypts was always strictly limited and Churchill established a routine for them to be evaluated and channelled directly to him and to a very tightly defined circle of senior staff.

Churchill was certainly among the first to appreciate the need for a proper system of evaluating the decrypts, but he was also in the habit of taking the information at face value and using it to harry his commanders. Initially, relevant data from Ultra was filtered through to General Wavell as if it were the product of unspecified intelligence sources. Increasingly, however, as Churchill wished to emphasize a point, he arranged for translations of complete texts to be passed to Wavell. This did not prevent Churchill from making his own interpretations of the German intentions and dispositions and pressing Wavell to take up the offensive prematurely, paying scant regard to the General's protestations.

By 1942 it had become impossible for Churchill personally to evaluate all the vast product of Ultra (3,000-4,000 decrypts per day by the middle of 1942[36]), and machinery for the more efficient assessment, communication and application of data was established. Churchill continued to use the data to cajole Auchinleck to take the offensive, though Auchinleck, using both Ultra data and other intelligence gathered in his theatre of war, made his own more sceptical assessment. Increasingly, as Hinsley argues, where Churchill went beyond 'bringing decrypts to the notice of the Chiefs of Staff or a theatre commander . . . to make a complaint or give an order, he . . . found that his initiative had either been anticipated or was resisted or went unheeded'.[37]

Ultra continued to be an immensely useful source throughout the campaigns in France, Belgium and Germany of 1944-1945 (**document 8**), providing increasingly rapid copies of German military plans, orders of battle and, significantly, German assessments of the Allies' intentions. It was a unique source and advantage to the Allies in the war, but, as with any intelligence data, from whatever reliable source, what mattered was its application and the degree to which it affected results.

Churchill and the strategic bombing offensive

Despite diminishing resources of material and personnel, Churchill had advocated the use of bombers to take the war to Germany as early as 14 September 1939, when he pressed for bombing raids to be conducted against 'strictly military objectives'.[38] Initially, the possible effects of German retaliation and American disapproval, combined with the need to husband resources for the anticipated German onslaught, made it necessary to postpone such raids. However, on 12 May 1940, the Cabinet at last freed itself of moral qualms and fears of American disapproval, arguing that the enemy had provided 'ample justification for retaliation on his country'.[39] As the final evacuations from Dunkirk were completed, Churchill's view was simple: 'An effort must be made to shake off the mental and moral prostration to the will and initiative of the enemy from which we suffer.'[40]

Even as early as July 1940 Churchill saw a bomber offensive against Germany as 'the one sure path'[41] to victory, and reiterated his belief in the primacy of air power in a memorandum of 6 March 1941 in which he claimed that it was

> impossible for the Army, except in resisting invasion, to play a primary role in the defeat of the enemy. The task can only be done by the staying power of the Navy, and above all by the effect of air predominance. Very valuable and important services may be rendered overseas by the Army in operations of a secondary order, and it is for these special operations that its organization and character should be adapted.[42]

His Director of Military Operations, Major-General Sir John Kennedy, later remarked: 'so sure was he of this that the bombing policy of the Air Staff was settled almost entirely by the Prime Minister himself in consultation with Portal, and was not controlled by the Chiefs of Staff', who, Kennedy claims, disagreed with Churchill's assessment.[43]

The scale of the Allied air raids over Germany increased steadily as production grew, and the technology and the skills of pilots and navigators improved. Because of the dangers from ground and enemy fighter defences, most air raids were conducted under protection of darkness, but this made identifying and hitting specific targets from 20,000 ft exceptionally difficult. While efforts continued to hit the industrial infrastructures that supported the German war effort, increasingly the technique that came to be applied was that of 'area bombing', whereby whole cities, rather than specific points, would be targeted. In July 1941 the Chiefs of Staff considered that 'a planned attack on civilian morale with the intensity and continuity which are essential if a final breakdown is to be produced' might 'make Germany sue for peace' and allow the British Army on the continent to become no more than an 'army of occupation'.[44]

Despite his earlier expression of faith in the strategic air offensive, while enemy fighter defences were still strong and industrial dispersal throughout the Reich made it impossible to bomb all industrial installations, Churchill retained a certain ambivalence about the effectiveness of area bombardment. In a note to the Chief of the Air Staff, Air Marshal Sir Charles Portal, in September 1941 he wrote: 'It is very disputable whether bombing by itself will be a decisive factor in the present war. On the contrary, all that we have learnt since the war began shows that its effects, both physical and moral, are greatly exaggerated.'[45]

The policy continued to be controversial. This is reflected in Churchill's draft memorandum of 28 March 1945 (**document 10**), in which he airs his serious doubts about the sense of continuing massive bombing of civilian targets at a time when the end of the war was in sight.

As Churchill anticipated, the German economy adapted extremely well, and German civilians scarcely exhibited any greater defeatism than the British had done during the Blitz. Whatever the faults of the policy of area bombing, though, it certainly helped national morale in Great Britain. At a time when Hitler was responding to the Allied invasion of France in June 1944 with daily raids of tens or even hundreds of V-weapons (**document 9**), Allied air raids on Germany gave the British people a feeling that they were at least giving the enemy as good as they were getting themselves. By the autumn of 1944, the Allies had achieved overwhelming air superiority against the *Luftwaffe*'s fighter force, thus ensuring the success of the strategic air offensive.

Churchill and the end of the war in Europe

In March 1945 the American Army crossed the Rhine at Remagen. Under an agreement reached between the American and British Allies, the thrust was to be towards Berlin. Without consulting the British, the Supreme Commander, US General Eisenhower, sent a telegram to Stalin to inform him of a revised strategy which was to take the American forces southwards to meet their Russian allies on the Elbe, entirely ruling out any possibility of the Anglo-American forces making for Berlin (**document 11**).

Churchill protested, but Eisenhower was intent on stopping the Anglo-American thrust at the Elbe and, with Roosevelt desperately ill (though the Prime Minister was unaware of this), Churchill could bring no influence to bear on the matter. The Grand Alliance was showing serious strains, as differences surfaced over proposals for the shape and political make-up of post-war eastern Europe and as Stalin openly flouted the agreements reached at Yalta in February.

At home, with the war in Europe over, Churchill hoped to sustain the coalition that had been in existence from May 1940 until victory had been achieved in the Far East. The main Labour members of the coalition, including the Deputy Prime Minister and Leader of the Labour Party, Clement Attlee, agreed in principle to continue, but the Labour Party conference voted, in Churchill's words, 'to set out upon the political warpath'[46] and call a general election, the first in the country for ten years. The election date was set for 5 July, although results were to be delayed for another three weeks beyond that to allow for the 'khaki' vote to be counted.

Meanwhile, the last of the conferences of the Grand Alliance was to be held at Potsdam, near Berlin. Churchill had invited Attlee to join him at the conference 'as a friend and counsellor, and help us on all the subjects on which we have been so long agreed'.[47] On 15 July Churchill flew to Berlin and two days later joined the first plenary session (**document 12**). The conference covered a broad range of subjects impinging on the post-war world, but in particular the terms of surrender for Japan, the future frontiers and government of Poland, reparations, and the future of the German economy.

Churchill returned with Attlee to London to be present for the declaration of the election results on 26 July. By lunch-time that day the hopes he had nurtured of a sizeable Conservative majority had faded and it was clear that the Labour Party, more obviously committed to social reform than the Tories, had won a landslide victory. After some deliberation Churchill decided to tender his resignation that evening. 'I have won the race - and now they have warned me off the turf',[48] he commented to those meeting him on his return from Buckingham Palace.

His formal statement which he sent to the press (**document 13**) could scarcely hide the sense of rejection that he felt from the 'ungrateful country' that he had languidly foreseen in the trenches. However, despite the overpowering gloom surrounding his sudden demise, his simple explanation of the situation to his personal map keeper, Captain Pim, demonstrated his adherence to the democratic principles that he had supported throughout his political career and especially through six years of war: 'They are perfectly entitled to vote as they please. This is democracy. This is what we've been fighting for.'[49]

Conclusion

In a lecture entitled 'Generals and Generalship', delivered at Trinity College, Cambridge, shortly before the outbreak of war in 1939, General Wavell concludes that a great leader 'must have "character", which simply means that he knows what he wants and has the courage and determination to get it. He should have a genuine interest in, and a real knowledge of, humanity . . . and, most vital of all, he must have what we call the fighting spirit, the will to win.' Finally, he adds, he must have 'one other moral quality', which he describes as 'a spirit of adventure, a touch of the gambler'. Wavell quotes Napoleon: 'If the art of war consisted merely in not taking risks glory would be at the mercy of very mediocre talent.'[50]

As he wrote this, one can almost imagine Wavell having in mind the figure of Churchill, for whom he had great admiration, despite the many differences between them. These words sum up the qualities that made Churchill a truly great leader, one who led his country to victory from a position, in 1940, which offered little hope that it could be achieved.

Churchill was a man willing to take chances and his Chiefs of Staff bore witness to his 'gambler' side. He was, furthermore, prepared to risk his own person in visits to the front and in the endless shuttle diplomacy necessary to sustain an alliance which included such diverse and powerful characters as Roosevelt, Stalin and de Gaulle. Not every venture could be a success and some historians harp on the failures. In doing so they often miss the crucial genius of Churchill that, as Wavell recognized, was necessary if victory was to be won. The Chiefs of Staff, senior commanders and even politicians of opposing parties agreed that he was the man for the hour. In the words of General Alan Brooke, he was simply 'the greatest war leader of our times, who guided this country from the very brink of the abyss of destruction to one of the most complete victories ever known in history'.[51]

Phil Reed, Curator, Cabinet War Rooms

Notes

1. Martin Gilbert, *Finest Hour: Winston S Churchill 1939-1941*, Heinemann, 1983, p 314
2. Winston Churchill, *The Gathering Storm*, Reprint Society Edition, 1950, p 532
3. Duff Cooper, *Old Men Forget*, Rupert Hart-Davis, 1953, p 256
4. Winston Churchill, *Gathering Storm*, p 330
5. Gilbert, *Finest Hour*, p 205
6. Gilbert, *Finest Hour*, p 286
7. John Wheeler-Bennett, *King George VI*, Macmillan, 1958, p 446
8. R W Thompson, *Generalissimo Churchill*, Scribner, 1973, p 18
9. W H Thompson, *I Was Churchill's Shadow*, Christopher Johnson, 1951, p 37
10. Hastings Ismay, *The Memoirs of Lord Ismay*, Heinemann, 1960, pp 146-147
11. Gilbert, *Finest Hour*, p 412
12. Ismay, *Memoirs*, p 156
13. Randolph S Churchill (ed), *Into Battle: Speeches by the Right Hon. Winston S Churchill*, Cassell, 1941, p 223
14. Randolph S Churchill, *Into Battle*, p 234
15. Gilbert, *Finest Hour*, p 548
16. Gilbert, *Finest Hour*, p 548
17. Joseph P Lash, *Roosevelt & Churchill 1939-1941*, André Deutsch, 1977, p 261
18. Gilbert, *Finest Hour*, p 937
19. Gilbert, *Finest Hour*, p 937
20. Charles Eade (ed), *The Unrelenting Struggle: War Speeches by the Right Hon. Winston S Churchill*, Cassell, 1942, p 63
21. Gilbert, *Finest Hour*, p 1274
22. Lash, *Roosevelt & Churchill*, p 492
23. Arthur Bryant, *The Turn of the Tide 1939-1943*, Collins, 1957, p 21
24. Winston Churchill, *Gathering Storm*, p 330
25. Chapter by Sir Ian Jacob in John Wheeler-Bennett (ed), *Action This Day: Working with Churchill*, Macmillan, 1968, p 198
26. John Connell, *Wavell: Scholar and Soldier*, Reprint Society Edition, 1966, p 256
27. Harold E Raugh, Jr, *Wavell in the Middle East 1939-1941*, Brassey's, 1993, p 109
28. Chapter by Jacob in Wheeler-Bennett, *Action This Day*, p 198
29. Bryant, *Turn of the Tide*, p 266
30. John Kennedy, *The Business of War*, Hutchinson, 1957, p 74
31. Ismay, *Memoirs*, pp 164-165
32. Ismay, *Memoirs*, p 159
33. Connell, *Wavell*, p 481
34. F H Hinsley, *British Intelligence in the Second World War*, abridged edn, HMSO, 1993, pp 216-217

35. F H Hinsley, 'Churchill and the Use of Special Intelligence' in Robert Blake and Wm Roger Louis (eds), *Churchill*, Oxford University Press, 1993, p 411
36. Hinsley, 'Churchill and the Use of Special Intelligence' in Blake and Louis, *Churchill*, p 422
37. Hinsley, 'Churchill and the Use of Special Intelligence' in Blake and Louis, *Churchill*, pp 422-423
38. Gilbert, *Finest Hour*, p 28
39. Gilbert, *Finest Hour*, p 329
40. Martin Gilbert, *Churchill: A Life*, Heinemann, 1991, p 655
41. Gilbert, *Churchill: A Life*, p 668
42. Kennedy, *Business of War*, p 97
43. Kennedy, *Business of War*, p 97
44. Michael Carver, 'Churchill and the Defence Chiefs' in Blake and Louis, *Churchill*, pp 367-368
45. Carver, 'Churchill and the Defence Chiefs' in Blake and Louis, *Churchill*, p 368
46. Charles Eade (ed), *Victory: War Speeches by the Right Hon. Winston S Churchill*, Cassell, 1946, p 186
47. Eade, *Victory*, p 212
48. Martin Gilbert, *Never Despair: Winston S Churchill 1945-1965*, Heinemann, 1988, p 109
49. Gilbert, *Never Despair*, p 111
50. A P Wavell, *The Good Soldier*, Macmillan, 1948, p 9
51. Arthur Bryant, *Triumph in the West 1943-1946*, Collins, 1959, p 482

Select bibliography

Addison, Paul. *Churchill on the Home Front 1900-1955*, Jonathan Cape, 1992

Blake, Robert, and Wm Roger Louis (eds). *Churchill*, Oxford University Press, 1993

Brendon, Piers. *Winston Churchill: An Authentic Hero*, Secker and Warburg, 1984

Bryant, Arthur. *The Turn of the Tide 1939-1943*, Collins, 1957

Bryant, Arthur. *Triumph in the West 1943-1946*, Collins, 1959

Cantwell, J D. *The Second World War. A Guide to Documents in the Public Record Office*, PRO Publications, 1998 (forthcoming)

Churchill, Winston. *The Second World War*, vols 1-6, Cassell, 1948-1954

Colville, John. *The Fringes of Power: Downing Street Diaries 1939-1955*, Hodder and Stoughton, 1985

Cooper, Duff. *Old Men Forget*, Rupert Hart-Davis, 1953

Edmonds, Robin. *The Big Three: Churchill, Roosevelt and Stalin in Peace and War*, Penguin, 1992

Gardner, Brian. *Churchill in His Time*, Methuen, 1968

Gilbert, Martin. *Finest Hour: Winston S Churchill 1939-1941*, Heinemann, 1983

Gilbert, Martin. *Road to Victory: Winston S Churchill 1941-1945*, Heinemann, 1986

Gilbert, Martin. *Never Despair: Winston S Churchill 1945-1965*, Heinemann, 1988

Hinsley, F H. *British Intelligence in the Second World War*, abridged edn, HMSO, 1993

Ismay, Hastings. *The Memoirs of Lord Ismay*, Heinemann, 1960

Keegan, John (ed). *Churchill's Generals*, Warner, 1992

Kennedy, John. *The Business of War*, Hutchinson, 1957

Lash, Joseph P. *Roosevelt & Churchill 1939-1941*, André Deutsch, 1977

Lewin, Ronald. *Ultra Goes to War: The Secret Story*, Hutchinson, 1978

Parrish, T (ed). *The Encyclopaedia of World War II*, Secker and Warburg, 1978

Thompson, R W. *Generalissimo Churchill*, Scribner, 1973

Wheeler-Bennett, John (ed). *Action This Day: Working with Churchill*, Macmillan, 1968

The documents

For an explanation of the document references, see the section 'The original documents' on p 19.

1. Churchill as John Bull: poster design

Original design by Illingworth for a poster depicting Churchill as John Bull, with his back to a wall over which troops from countries of the British Commonwealth and Empire are clambering to assist him. This image personifies the 'never surrender' spirit so closely associated with Winston Churchill in the dark days of 1940, following the fall of France. It comes from record class INF 3, which contains original paintings and drawings produced through the Ministry of Information for propaganda and publicity purposes between 1939 and 1946.

c. 1940   PRO reference - **INF 3/1325**

2. Letter from Robert Boothby to Churchill

In this handwritten letter Robert Boothby sets out the situation in the House of Commons on 9 May 1940, the day before Churchill became Prime Minister.

Boothby was a back-bench Conservative MP who had served as Churchill's Parliamentary Private Secretary when he was Chancellor of the Exchequer. He was also one of a small number of Conservatives who had opposed the government's policy of appeasement in the late 1930s.

Boothby's letter captures the mood of the House on the eve of Neville Chamberlain's resignation. He confirms that neither the Labour Party under Clement Attlee nor the Liberal Party under Archibald Sinclair are prepared to support Chamberlain, and lists the group of Conservative MPs who are calling for a change in leadership. He also claims that a majority in Parliament are now in favour of 'radical reconstruction'. This will involve the removal of two of the ministers most clearly associated with appeasement: Sir John Simon, the Chancellor of the Exchequer, and Sir Samuel Hoare, the Secretary of State for Air.

Churchill's main rival for the premiership was the Foreign Secretary, Lord Halifax. In a postscript to this letter, written later in the day, Boothby added that he had heard that the Labour Party leadership would not serve under Halifax. Events were clearly moving in Churchill's favour, but he was not the 'inevitable' Prime Minister until Halifax ruled himself out of the running at a private meeting with Churchill and Chamberlain at Downing Street on the very afternoon that this letter was written.

The letter provides a vivid insight into the political machinations which culminated in Churchill's appointment as Prime Minister. He was not elected to the office by the public; he was not even the leader of a political party; but he was the man most capable of uniting the various factions in Parliament and providing them with true leadership.

9 May 1940   Churchill Papers - **CHAR 2/392B/146**

3. 'Never in the field of human conflict' speech

In this wide-ranging examination of the war situation, delivered in the House of Commons on 20 August 1940 and broadcast later that day, Churchill compares the current conflict with the opening phase of the First World War, and discusses the fall of France, British military strength, and co-operation with the United States. But this speech is now principally remembered for its stirring account of the role of the Royal Air Force in the Battle of Britain, and for one key phrase in particular.

The *Luftwaffe* required aerial supremacy over England as a precursor to possible invasion. On 13 August, code-named 'Eagle Day', the German air force launched its major offensive. However, 1,485 sorties resulted in the destruction of a mere 13 British fighters, with the *Luftwaffe* losing 45 aircraft. Three days later Churchill followed the battle in the skies above from the Operations Room of No 11 Group, Fighter Command, at Uxbridge. During the journey back to his official country residence, Chequers, he confided to his Chief of Staff, General Sir Hastings Ismay, that he had 'never been so moved' and uttered the immortal tribute to the RAF pilots, which he repeated four days later in a speech delivered in the House of Commons: 'Never in the field of human conflict was so much owed by so many to so few.'

This sentence, which Churchill had long mulled over in various forms, illustrates the unique power of his oratory. Violet Asquith, Churchill's lifelong friend and daughter of the former Prime Minister, commented: 'nothing so simple, so majestic and so true has been said in so great a moment of human history'. It is located in the opening paragraph of the fifth page of this contemporary edition of the speech taken from *Hansard's Parliamentary Debates*.

20 August 1940   PRO reference - **ZHC 2/873**

4. Letter from President Roosevelt to Churchill

Churchill and President Franklin Roosevelt maintained regular contact by letter and telegram from the outbreak of the war. Only days after Hitler's invasion of Poland in September 1939, Roosevelt wrote to Churchill as First Lord of the Admiralty asking him to 'keep me in touch personally with anything you want me to know about'. He also harked back to their common experience of the First World War when FDR was Assistant Secretary of the Navy and Churchill had served his initial stint as First Lord of the Admiralty. Although Roosevelt pledged to keep America out of the war when he was elected for an unprecedented third term in 1940, he realized that the world could only be made safe by the defeat of the Axis powers. During 1940 agreements enabled aircraft and munitions for Britain to be manufactured in the United States, and the loan of American ships was negotiated, though Britain's limited financial resources remained a problem. In January 1941 Harry Hopkins arrived in London as Roosevelt's emissary, and helped initiate the Lend-Lease agreement, by which the United States would supply Britain's military needs while payment was deferred until the end of hostilities.

On the day joint Anglo-American staff talks began in Washington (27 January 1941), Churchill lunched in London with Roosevelt's recent opponent for the presidency, Wendell Willkie, who brought Churchill a letter from FDR. The envelope was addressed to 'A Certain Naval Person' (Churchill's code-name for himself). The letter inside read:

> Dear Churchill
> Wendell Willkie will give you this. He is truly helping to keep politics out over here.
> I think this verse applies to your people as it does to us:
>
>> 'Sail on, Oh Ship of State!
>> Sail on Oh Union strong and great
>> Humanity with all its fears,
>> With all the hope of future years
>> Is hanging breathless on thy fate'
>
> As ever yours
> Franklin D Roosevelt

Churchill telegraphed Roosevelt the next day stating that he 'was deeply moved by the verse of Longfellow's which you had quoted. I shall have it framed as a souvenir of these tremendous days, as a mark of our friendly relations, which have been built up telegraphically but also telepathically under all the stresses.' Churchill was true to his word and the framed letter and envelope hung for many years in his beloved home, Chartwell in Kent. Its prolonged exposure to sunlight accounts for the faded appearance. The paper colour would originally have been official White House light green.

20 January 1941   Churchill Additional Papers - **WCHL 13/1**

5. Letter from Clementine Churchill to her husband

On 4 August 1941 Churchill left Scapa Flow in the Orkney Islands on board HMS *Prince of Wales* for a secret destination. Five days later he reached Placentia Bay in Newfoundland, the location of his first face-to-face meeting with President Roosevelt during the war. Clementine Churchill was one of only a handful of people to know her husband's precise whereabouts, which were a source of much public debate in Britain, as Clementine recounts in the second page of her letter. On 11 August talks began between President and Prime Minister, as well as the Chiefs of Staff and diplomats. As a consequence the United States agreed to provide aid to the Soviet Union, to increase military supplies to Britain, and to take an enhanced role in protecting North Atlantic convoys. Furthermore, Japan was warned over its policy in the south-west Pacific. It was at this meeting that the 'Atlantic Charter' was formulated. Under its terms Britain and America pledged to 'respect the right of all peoples to choose the form of government under which they will live'. Clementine is referring to the Charter when she writes of the joint statement by Deputy Prime Minister Clement Attlee and the White House on the first page of this letter and in its postscript.

At the time of writing Clementine was away from London in a country 'retreat'. The strains of public life had taken their toll, and she used the opportunity of Winston's absence to spend ten days at Dr Lief's health establishment at Tring in Hertfordshire. The style of this letter is typical of the correspondence between wife and husband throughout the war. Clementine shows her concern for the success of Winston's voyage in the third page, hoping 'that you and the President like each other'. She had no need to worry. On his return from Newfoundland, Churchill told the War Cabinet that he had 'established warm and deep personal relations with our great friend' and that Roosevelt had 'made it clear' to him that he 'would look for an "incident" which would justify him opening hostilities'.

Though they did discuss the momentous events in which Churchill was involved, most of Clementine and Winston's wartime correspondence concentrates on personal and family matters. Here Clementine writes about her engagements, mentioning lunch with Walter Moyne (then Secretary of State for the Colonies and a family friend). The humorous account of the activities of the local Home Guard is also typical of the light nature of their letters even during the most anxious of times. Clementine's signing-off is again characteristic. She would often accompany her signature with a drawing of a cat and would on occasion call herself 'kat'; Churchill was her 'pug dog', and their children a litter of 'kittens'.

14 August 1941   Baroness Spencer-Churchill Papers - **CSCT 1/25**

6. Cabinet War Room record

Intelligence summaries of events in each theatre of the war were produced every day by the Central Map Room for the information of the War Cabinet and the Chiefs of Staff, while one copy was delivered by the Duty Officer each morning to Buckingham Palace for the King. This one, dated 8 December 1941, announces the commencement of hostilities with Japan after Imperial forces had invaded the British colony of Malaya and attacked the American naval base at Pearl Harbour. These events marked a watershed in the world conflict. Churchill later reflected in a secret minute to the Foreign Secretary, Anthony Eden (dated 19 September 1943):

It was, however, a blessing that Japan attacked the United States and this brought America wholeheartedly into the war. Greater good fortune has rarely happened to the British Empire than this event which has revealed our friends and foes in their true light, and may lead, through the merciless crushing of Japan, to a new relationship of immense benefit to the English-speaking countries and to the whole world.

(PRO reference - PREM 3/158/4)

Other information in this summary records all air activity (including tonnage of bombs dropped by the Royal Air Force), the successful link up of Commonwealth forces ending the siege of Tobruk (which was to fall to the Germans in June 1942, only to be recaptured in November 1942), and the continued fighting between Russian and German armies at the gates of Moscow.

8 December 1941   PRO reference - **CAB 100/8**

7. Telegram from Churchill in Egypt to the Deputy Prime Minister and War Cabinet

In August 1942 Churchill, aged sixty-seven, left Whitehall and undertook a gruelling and dangerous tour which took him close to some of the main theatres of war. Between 12 and 16 August he held his first, crucial, face-to-face meeting with Stalin in Moscow. But he also felt it necessary to hold discussions with his military commanders in the Middle East and spent several days in Egypt both before and after this trip to the Soviet Union.

Churchill's decision to visit the Middle East in person reflects his growing unease over the lack of offensive spirit being shown by the British commanders in the desert. In July there had been a motion of no confidence in the central direction of the war in Parliament. Although it was easily defeated, this, combined with losses in the Far East and renewed offensives by Rommel in north Africa, can only have served to increase the pressure on Churchill to deliver a military victory.

In this telegram to the War Cabinet Churchill summarizes the changes in the military command which resulted from his visits. Lieutenant-General B L Montgomery was now to command the Eighth Army, while General Harold Alexander replaced General Claude Auchinleck as the overall Commander-in-Chief in the Middle East. The document goes on to talk about the forthcoming battle with Rommel, and illustrates Churchill's grasp of the details of troop dispositions and armaments. Churchill's obvious confidence in the new leadership was later to be vindicated by success at the Battle of El Alamein (23 October - 4 November 1942), although some historians have argued that this victory owed much to the preparations made by Auchinleck.

The telegram contains a couple of code-names. 'Torch' was the Allied invasion of north-west Africa, which took place on 8 November 1942. 'Jubilee' refers to the unsuccessful amphibious raid on Dieppe in August 1942, which ended in the loss of many Canadian and British lives.

21 August 1942   Churchill Papers - **CHAR 20/87/68-70**

8. Ultra decrypt of German signals intelligence

The German armed forces encoded their intelligence signals using the sophisticated 'Enigma' cipher machine, each service having its own versions and settings. 'Ultra' was one of the code-names given to Enigma signals that were intercepted and decrypted at the Government Code and Cipher School (GCCS) at Bletchley Park, then known as 'Station X'. The cryptographers owed much of their success to the capture, quite early in the war, of the vital wheels of a German Enigma encoding machine and subsequently of code-books from a sunken U-boat, as well as to the development of a primitive computer, known as 'Colossus', at Bletchley Park itself.

At first, Ultra decrypts were circulated as if they were reports from British secret agents, using the standard MI6 preamble 'CX'. The letters 'CX/MSS' on the right-hand side of the first page of this document indicate that the information is to be forwarded to Washington.

Churchill (or, in his absence, either the Lord Privy Seal or the Deputy Prime Minister) was sent daily summaries of chosen Enigma messages. The selection usually had three main elements (European military operations, naval headlines, and diplomatic intercepts) as well as a cover note from 'C' (the head of the Secret Intelligence Service who was also Director of GCCS).

This Ultra decrypt reports, from the German perspective, the progress being made by the Allied invasion armies on D-Day, 6 June 1944.

Explanation of the entries:

(A) & (B) Asnelles and Arromanches were on 'Gold' beach in the Anglo-Canadian sector.

(C) The Vire estuary was just to the south of 'Utah' beach, in the American sector and on the western flank of the D-Day invasion.

(D) Marcouf was also in the 'Utah' beach area, where there was a heavy naval battery of three 21 cm guns which overlooked the invasion area. Despite repeated Allied attacks, the battery held out for five days until the defenders evacuated.

(E) Barfleur was on the northern tip of the Cotentin peninsula, and had a heavy naval battery of three 17 cm guns. Since this battery had a commanding field of fire over the invasion shipping area, its destruction was a high priority for the Allied naval gunners.

Ultra decrypts remained a closely guarded secret, not mentioned even in official war histories until the publication of *The Ultra Secret* by F W Winterbotham in 1974. Ironically, he was the officer charged with keeping their existence hidden during the war. The first transfer of Ultra decrypts to the Public Record Office was not made until 1993, where they are to be found in the HW classes of records.

6 June 1944   PRO reference - **HW 1/2893**

9. Minutes of War Cabinet meeting: WM (44) 95th Conclusions

The War Cabinet met regularly in the Cabinet War Rooms throughout the Blitz and during the V-weapon raids of 1944 and 1945. It comprised only a small number of ministers, but was supplemented by other ministers, key officials and military men as required by the business in hand. Its minutes, known as 'Conclusions', were printed for limited circulation. Certain conclusions were regarded as being especially secret and were recorded in the Cabinet Secretary's standard file as 'confidential annexes', such as those on Russo-Polish relations in the section on 'Foreign Affairs' on the fourth side of this document.

This example illustrates the wide variety of issues that arose for consideration at War Cabinet level, ranging across all theatres and all aspects of the global conflict. In July 1944 matters under examination included: the urgent threat posed by the V-1 flying bombs (pilotless aircraft) and the joint Anglo-American operation code-named 'Crossbow' to bomb the V-weapon sites; the progress of the Allied Expeditionary Force in Normandy, code-named 'Overlord', including evidence of war crimes committed by the *Waffen SS* against Canadian and British prisoners of war; and reports of the attempted assassination of Hitler by Colonel Count Claus von Stauffenberg.

24 July 1944   PRO reference - **CAB 65/43**

10. Minute from Churchill to Chiefs of Staff on Allied bombing policy

The bombing of Dresden in February 1945 has been compared by some to the dropping of the atomic bomb on Hiroshima. During January 1945 the renewed Russian offensive looked as if it would bring a speedy end to the war and the Germans were rushing up reinforcements from the west. At the Yalta Conference of Allied leaders in February 1945 General Antonov, Deputy Chief of Staff of the Red Army, had asked that Anglo-American strategic air forces assist the Soviets with 'air attacks against communications' and that, in particular, they 'should paralyse the centres: Berlin and Leipzig'. Bomber Command's raid on Dresden with 805 bombers took place on the night of 13-14 February, and was immediately followed up by heavy daylight raids by 600 bombers of the US Eighth Air Force on the 14th and 15th. Estimates as to the numbers that died in the ensuing fire-storms vary from 25,000 to 135,000, compared to the 70,000 to 80,000 who died at Hiroshima.

This minute to Ismay was composed a month after the Dresden raid and was intended for the Chiefs of Staff Committee. It reveals Churchill's personal reservations about continuing the policy of large-scale bombing of cities, not least on the practical grounds that conquering a wasteland would create major problems in itself for the occupying power. He candidly admits that some bombing operations had been launched, 'though under other pretexts', simply for the sake of increasing the terror. It is interesting to note that Air Marshal Sir Charles Portal, the Chief of the Air Staff, persuaded Churchill to withdraw this minute. The redrafted version omits the reference to terror and begins instead with the less controversial phrase, 'It seems to me that the moment has come when the question of the so called "area bombing" of German cities should be reviewed from the point of view of our own interests.'

28 March 1945   PRO reference - **CAB 120/303**

11. Telegram from Churchill to General Eisenhower on the desirability of taking Berlin

By the end of March 1945 Germany was beaten and her imminent military collapse was expected. Soviet forces were advancing rapidly on Germany from the east. Having captured Warsaw in January and Budapest in February, the Red Army was now poised for a final push towards Berlin. The chances of American and British forces also entering Berlin had seemed good until General Eisenhower's decision on 30 March to advance in a more southerly direction, through Leipzig to Dresden.

Churchill and the British Chiefs of Staff had several reasons for opposing Eisenhower's new strategy, which they set out in this telegram. They felt it would leave the 21st Army Group, containing the British forces under Field Marshal Montgomery, away from the main action. But they also recognized the huge political advantage to be gained from taking Berlin. The capture of the German capital would be a major psychological blow to the enemy and would counter the Soviet claim that they had done all the real fighting and destroyed the Third Reich single-handedly.

Then there were the post-war strategic considerations, especially the threat that Churchill saw being posed by Soviet expansionism. There were already worrying signs that the Red Army would not be prepared to relinquish existing gains in eastern Europe.

31 March 1945   PRO reference - **CAB 120/422**

12. Churchill's Allied Expeditionary Force permit

The defeat of Hitler's Third Reich left much of western Europe under the occupation of General Eisenhower's Allied Expeditionary Force. Churchill, who had not enjoyed a proper holiday since becoming Prime Minister, flew to southern France on 7 July and spent a week painting at the Château de Bordaberry. On 15 July he travelled directly on to Berlin to take part in the final summit meeting with President Truman and Marshal Stalin at Potsdam.

Travel through war-torn Europe was now carefully controlled and even the Prime Minister needed an official permit to enter Berlin. Peter Carlos Clarke, the issuing officer, sent a handwritten letter to the Prime Minister's Private Secretary asking whether he might have the permit returned to him, once Churchill had no further use for it, 'as a memento of the momentous times we have gone, and are going through at this period in our history'. It seems unlikely that there were two permits, and it must therefore be concluded that, for whatever reasons, this request was not granted. The permit survives in the Churchill Papers in a box with other similar souvenirs, suggesting that perhaps Churchill wanted to keep it for his own scrapbook.

Two interesting observations can be made about this permit. First, it was valid for repeated trips abroad until 4 October, and so would have enabled Churchill to attend the whole of the Potsdam Conference had he won the July 1945 general election. Second, it was never signed. While we cannot be certain of the reason for this, the most likely explanation is that Churchill was simply too busy. Besides, who was going to question his identity?

4 July 1945   Churchill Papers - **CHUR 1/104B**

13. Churchill's statement of resignation

There can be no doubt that Churchill was personally extremely popular in July 1945 and expected to win the general election. Yet his preoccupation with victory at all costs had blinded him to the changing political mood at home. After almost six years of war and sacrifice, the electorate wanted peace and social reform.

Polling took place on 5 July, but the need to count the service votes meant that the results were not announced until the 26th. The Labour Party won a landslide victory, gaining an absolute majority of 146. Churchill acted swiftly, travelling to Buckingham Palace to tender his resignation to the King before issuing a public statement. This is the text that he approved, which has been initialled and dated by him.

This defeat was a bitter blow to Churchill. Clementine, who wanted him to retire from politics, suggested that it was perhaps a blessing in disguise, to which Churchill memorably replied that the blessing was certainly very effectively disguised. The official resignation statement is more measured, but clearly shows his regret at not being permitted to finish the job. His comment that results against Japan 'may come much quicker than we have hitherto been entitled to expect' may be an oblique reference to the existence of the atomic bomb. Churchill had been informed of the successful testing of this awesome weapon only days earlier at Potsdam.

26 July 1945   Churchill Papers - **CHAR 20/195A/79**

Introductory text © Trustees of the Imperial War Museum 1998; document descriptions © Crown copyright 1998

The original documents

The Churchill Archives Centre (CAC) - documents 2, 4, 5, 7, 12 and 13

Located within the grounds of Churchill College, Cambridge, itself the national and commonwealth memorial to Sir Winston, Churchill Archives Centre currently holds over four hundred collections relating to the Churchill era and beyond.

The **Churchill Papers** are the personal archive of Sir Winston Churchill. This huge collection, comprising an estimated one million pieces of paper, reflects all aspects of Churchill's life from his childhood letters and school reports to his final writings. There is a mass of wartime material, including Churchill's personal correspondence and his private copies of official minutes and telegrams. This collection was purchased for the nation using a grant from the Heritage Lottery Fund in April 1995, and is now administered by the Sir Winston Churchill Archive Trust.

The Churchill Papers are complemented by a range of other collections. The papers of his wife, Clementine (the **Baroness Spencer-Churchill Papers**), provide a window into the private life of the war leader. The **Churchill Additional Papers** include the handwritten letter from President Roosevelt. Both of these collections are administered by Churchill College.

Anyone interested in viewing these collections should write to: The Archivist, Churchill Archives Centre, Churchill College, Cambridge, CB3 0DS; tel: 01223 336 087. Web site address: http://www.chu.cam.ac.uk/archives/home.htm

The Imperial War Museum

The Imperial War Museum was founded in 1917 and records all aspects of military operations in which Great Britain or the Commonwealth have been involved since 1914. This is achieved with the aid of its extensive galleries in Lambeth Road, London; its Battle of Britain and later USAAF airfield at Duxford, Cambridgeshire; the Second World War cruiser HMS *Belfast*, moored on the Thames; and Churchill's underground HQ, the Cabinet War Rooms. The Museum also holds the national collections of film, photographs and art relating to twentieth-century conflict, as well as unique collections of printed sources, documents and sound recordings. All the Museum's displays and reference collections are open to the public and an active education service operates at each site. A permanent exhibition on Winston Churchill in the Second World War, featuring papers from the Churchill Archives Centre collections, can be seen at the Cabinet War Rooms in Horse Guards Road, London, SW1A 2AQ; tel: 0171 930 6961. Web site address: http://www.iwm.org.uk/

The Public Record Office - documents 1, 3, 6, 8, 9, 10 and 11

The Public Record Office is the repository of the national archives for England, Wales and the United Kingdom. Founded in 1838 to bring together and preserve the records of central government and the courts of law, and to make them available to all who wish to consult them, it is the treasure house of the nation's memory. The records span an unbroken period from the eleventh century to the present day, and may be seen by anyone holding a valid reader's ticket, issued on proof of identity. The PRO is an invaluable resource for academic researchers, local historians, genealogists and many other groups of readers. For further information on PRO services, contact: Public Record Office, Ruskin Avenue, Kew, Richmond, Surrey, TW9 4DU; tel: 0181 392 5200. Web site address: http://www.pro.gov.uk/

Acknowledgements

Grateful thanks are due to the help provided by the Lady Soames, DBE; to the Master and Fellows of Churchill College for permission to use the letter from President Roosevelt (document 4); and to Lady Boothby (document 2). Documents 6-13 are Crown copyright and reproduced by permission of the Controller of HMSO. Document 1 supplied by the PRO Image Library.

Document 2:   © The Estate of Lord Boothby, courtesy of Lady Boothby
Document 5:   © The Master and Fellows of Churchill College, Cambridge

Cover illustrations

Front cover: Official Canadian military photograph, c. 1945, Churchill Papers - CHUR 1/103

Inside front cover: Churchill and his wife, Clementine, in a launch on the Thames *en route* to inspect bomb damage in London's dockland on 25 September 1940, ref: H 4367 © IWM, courtesy of the Trustees of the Imperial War Museum; quote from Churchill's speech at the Mansion House, London, 10 November 1942

Inside pocket: Churchill on board the British destroyer HMS *Kelvin*, crossing the English Channel to France on 12 June 1944, six days after D-Day, ref: EA 26238 © IWM, courtesy of the Trustees of the Imperial War Museum; Winston Churchill as drawn by the cartoonist Ralph Sallon © Ralph Sallon

A Teacher's Guide to accompany this pack will be available to educational establishments from the Public Record Office shop, or can be ordered from Sales and Marketing, Public Record Office, Ruskin Avenue, Kew, Richmond, Surrey, TW9 4DU; tel: 0181 392 5271; e-mail: bookshop@pro.gov.uk

THE CHARTWELL TRUST

Mr. R. Boothby

Private & Confidential.

Dear Winston.

I have been in the House all day.

This is the situation, as I see it.

(1) The Labour party won't touch Chamberlain, at any price.

(2) Nor will Archie

(3) Nor will our group.

Therefore it is inconceivable that Chamberlain can carry through a reconstruction of the Government.

A majority of the House is, nevertheless, determined on a __radical__ reconstruction, which will involve ("inter alia") the elimination of Simon and Hoare.

(4) Opinion is hardening against Halifax ~~too~~ as Prime Minister.

I am doing my best to foster this, because I cannot feel he is, in any circumstances, the right man.

At the moment of writing, our group would oppose his appointment, unless it commanded universal assent.

It is quite a powerful group. It is now led by Amery; and includes Duff Cooper, Eddie Winterton, Belisha, Hammersley,

(OVER

Dick Law,

Harold Macmillan, Henderson Stewart, Emrys Evans, Mrs. Tate, R. Tree, Russell, Harold Nicolson, Gunston, Clem Davies, & King-Hall.

At a meeting held this afternoon, at which all the above were present, it was unanimously agreed:—

(a) That there must be a genuine National Government, comprised of all parties;

(b) That the Prime Minister, whoever he may be, should choose his colleagues on grounds of merit alone, without undue reference to the various Whips' Offices. For this reason it was felt that it would be an advantage rather than a handicap that the War Premier should not himself be a party leader;

(c) That we would give full support to any Prime Minister who could form such a Government, and none to one who could'nt.

In fact, I find a gathering concensus of opinion in all quarters that you are the necessary and inevitable Prime Minister — as I wrote to you some weeks ago.

God knows it is a terrible prospect for you.

But I don't see how you can avoid it.

Yours ever
Bob.

WAR SITUATION.

3.52 p.m.

The Prime Minister (Mr. Churchill):
Almost a year has passed since the war began, and it is natural for us, I think, to pause on our journey at this milestone and survey the dark, wide field. It is also useful to compare the first year of this second war against German aggression with its forerunner a quarter of a century ago. Although this war is in fact only a continuation of the last, very great differences in its character are apparent. In the last war millions of men fought by hurling enormous masses of steel at one another. " Men and shells " was the cry, and prodigious slaughter was the consequence. In this war nothing of this kind has yet appeared. It is a conflict of strategy, of organisation, of technical apparatus, of science, mechanics and morale. The British casualties in the first 12 months of the Great War amounted to 365,000. In this war, I am thankful to say, British killed, wounded, prisoners and missing, including civilians, do not exceed 92,000, and of these a large proportion are alive as prisoners of war. Looking more widely around, one may say that throughout all Europe for one man killed or wounded in the first year perhaps five were killed or wounded in 1914-15.

The slaughter is but a fraction, but the consequences to the belligerents have been even more deadly. We have seen great countries with powerful armies dashed out of coherent existence in a few weeks. We have seen the French Republic and the renowned French Army beaten into complete and total submission with less than the casualties which they suffered in any one of half-a-dozen of the battles of 1914-18. The entire body—it might almost seem at times the soul—of France has succumbed to physical effects incomparably less terrible than those which were sustained with fortitude and undaunted will power 25 years ago. Although up to the present the loss of life has been mercifully diminished, the decisions reached in the course of the struggle are even more profound upon the fate of nations than anything that has ever happened since barbaric times. Moves are made upon the scientific and strategic boards, advantages are gained by mechanical means, as a result of which scores of millions of men become incapable of further resistance, or judge themselves incapable of further resistance, and a fearful game of chess proceeds from check to mate by which the unhappy players seem to be inexorably bound.

There is another more obvious difference from 1914. The whole of the warring nations are engaged, not only soldiers, but the entire population, men, women and children. The fronts are everywhere. The trenches are dug in the towns and streets. Every village is fortified. Every road is barred. The front line runs through the factories. The workmen are soldiers with different weapons but the same courage. These are great and distinctive changes from what many of us saw in the struggle of a quarter of a century ago. There seems to be every reason to believe that this new kind of war is well suited to the genius and the resources of the British nation and the British Empire and that, once we get properly equipped and properly started, a war of this kind will be more favourable to us than the sombre mass slaughters of the Somme and Passchendaele. If it is a case of the whole nation fighting and suffering together, that ought to suit us, because we are the most united of all the nations, because we entered the war upon the national will and with our eyes open, and because we have been nurtured in freedom and individual responsibility and are the products, not of totalitarian uniformity but of tolerance and variety. If all these qualities are turned, as they are being turned, to the arts of war, we may be able to show the enemy quite a lot of things that they have not thought of yet. Since the Germans drove the Jews out and lowered their technical standards, our science is definitely ahead of theirs. Our geographical position, the command of the sea, and the friendship of the United States enable us to draw resources from the whole world and to manufacture weapons of war of every kind, but especially of the superfine kinds, on a scale hitherto practised only by Nazi Germany.

Hitler is now sprawled over Europe. Our offensive springs are being slowly compressed, and we must resolutely and methodically prepare ourselves for the campaigns of 1941 and 1942. Two or three years are not a long time, even in our short, precarious lives. They are nothing in the history of the nation, and when we are doing the finest thing in the world, and have the honour to be the sole champion of the liberties of all Europe, we must not grudge these years or weary as we toil and struggle through them. It does not follow that our energies in future years will be exclusively confined to defending ourselves and our possessions. Many opportunities may lie open to amphibious power, and we must be ready to take advantage of them. One of the ways to bring this war to a speedy end is to convince the enemy, not by words but by deeds, that we have both the will and the means, not only to go on indefinitely but to strike heavy and unexpected blows. The road to victory may not be so long as we expect. But we have no right to count upon this. Be it long or short, rough or smooth, we mean to reach our journey's end.

It is our intention to maintain and enforce a strict blockade not only of Germany but of Italy, France and all the other countries that have fallen into the German power. I read in the papers that Herr Hitler has also proclaimed a strict blockade of the British Islands. No one can complain of that. I remember the Kaiser doing it in the last war. What indeed would be a matter of general complaint would be if we were to prolong the agony of all Europe by allowing food to come in to nourish the Nazis and aid their war effort, or to allow food to go in to the subjugated peoples, which certainly would be pillaged off them by their Nazi conquerors.

There have been many proposals, founded on the highest motives, that food should be allowed to pass the blockade for the relief of these populations. I regret that we must refuse these requests. The Nazis declare that they have created a new unified economy in Europe. They have repeatedly stated that they possess ample reserves of food and that they can feed their captive peoples. In a German broadcast of 27th June it was said that while Mr. Hoover's plan for relieving France, Belgium and Holland deserved commendation, the German forces had already taken the necessary steps. We know that in Norway when the German troops went in, there were food supplies to last for a year. We know that Poland though not a rich

country usually produces sufficient food for her people. Moreover, the other countries which Herr Hitler has invaded all held considerable stocks when the Germans entered and are themselves, in many cases, very substantial food producers. If all this food is not available now, it can only be because it has been removed to feed the people of Germany and to give them increased rations—for a change —during the last few months. At this season of the year and for some months to come, there is the least chance of scarcity as the harvest has just been gathered in. The only agencies which can create famine in any part of Europe now and during the coming winter, will be German exactions or German failure to distribute the supplies which they command.

There is another aspect. Many of the most valuable foods are essential to the manufacture of vital war material. Fats are used to make explosives. Potatoes make the alcohol for motor spirit. The plastic materials now so largely used in the construction of aircraft are made of milk. If the Germans used these commodities to help them to bomb our women and children, rather than to feed the populations who produce them, we may be sure that imported foods would go the same way, directly or indirectly, or be employed to relieve the enemy of the responsibilities he has so wantonly assumed. Let Hitler bear his responsibilities to the full and let the peoples of Europe who groan beneath his yoke aid in every way the coming of the day when that yoke will be broken. Meanwhile, we can and we will arrange in advance for the speedy entry of food into any part of the enslaved area, when this part has been wholly cleared of German forces, and has genuinely regained its freedom. We shall do our best to encourage the building up of reserves of food all over the world, so that there will always be held up before the eyes of the peoples of Europe, including—I say it deliberately —the German and Austrian peoples, the certainty that the shattering of the Nazi power will bring to them all immediate food, freedom and peace.

Rather more than a quarter of a year has passed since the new Government came into power in this country. What a cataract of disaster has poured out upon us since then. The trustful Dutch over-

[The Prime Minister.]
whelmed; their beloved and respected Sovereign driven into exile; the peaceful city of Rotterdam the scene of a massacre as hideous and brutal as anything in the Thirty Years' War. Belgium invaded and beaten down; our own fine Expeditionary Force, which King Leopold called to his rescue, cut off and almost captured, escaping as it seemed only by a miracle and with the loss of all its equipment; our Ally, France, out; Italy in against us; all France in the power of the enemy, all its arsenals and vast masses of military material converted or convertible to the enemy's use; a puppet Government set up at Vichy which may at any moment be forced to become our foe; the whole Western seaboard of Europe from the North Cape to the Spanish frontier in German hands; all the ports, all the airfields on this immense front, employed against us as potential springboards of invasion. Moreover, the German air power, numerically so far outstripping ours, has been brought so close to our Island that what we used to dread greatly has come to pass and the hostile bombers not only reach our shores in a few minutes and from many directions, but can be escorted by their fighting aircraft. Why Sir, if we had been confronted at the beginning of May with such a prospect, it would have seemed incredible that at the end of a period of horror and disaster, or at this point in a period of horror and disaster, we should stand erect, sure of ourselves, masters of our fate and with the conviction of final victory burning unquenchable in our hearts. Few would have believed we could survive; none would have believed that we should to-day not only feel stronger but should actually be stronger than we have ever been before.

Let us see what has happened on the other side of the scales. The British nation and the British Empire finding themselves alone, stood undismayed against disaster. No one flinched or wavered; nay, some who formerly thought of peace, now think only of war. Our people are united and resolved, as they have never been before. Death and ruin have become small things compared with the shame of defeat or failure in duty. We cannot tell what lies ahead. It may be that even greater ordeals lie before us. We shall face whatever is coming to us. We are sure of ourselves and of our cause

and here then is the supreme fact which has emerged in these months of trial.

Meanwhile, we have not only fortified our hearts but our Island. We have rearmed and rebuilt our armies in a degree which would have been deemed impossible a few months ago. We have ferried across the Atlantic, in the month of July, thanks to our friends over there, an immense mass of munitions of all kinds, cannon, rifles, machine-guns, cartridges and shell, all safely landed without the loss of a gun or a round. The output of our own factories, working as they have never worked before, has poured forth to the troops. The whole British Army is at home. More than 2,000,000 determined men have rifles and bayonets in their hands to-night and three-quarters of them are in regular military formations. We have never had armies like this in our Island in time of war. The whole Island bristles against invaders, from the sea or from the air. As I explained to the House in the middle of June, the stronger our Army at home, the larger must the invading expedition be, and the larger the invading expedition, the less difficult will be the task of the Navy in detecting its assembly and in intercepting and destroying it on passage; and the greater also would be the difficulty of feeding and supplying the invaders if ever they landed, in the teeth of continuous naval and air attack on their communications. All this is classical and venerable doctrine. As in Nelson's day, the maxim holds, "Our first line of defence is the enemy's ports." Now air reconnaissance and photography have brought to an old principle a new and potent aid.

Our Navy is far stronger than it was at the beginning of the war. The great flow of new construction set on foot at the outbreak, is now beginning to come in. We hope our friends across the ocean will send us a timely reinforcement to bridge the gap between the peace flotillas of 1939 and the war flotillas of 1941. There is no difficulty in sending such aid. The seas and oceans are open. The U-boats are contained. The magnetic mine is, up to the present time, effectively mastered. The merchant tonnage under the British flag, after a year of unlimited U-boat war, after eight months of intensive mining attack, is larger than when we began. We have, in addition, under our control at least 4,000,000 tons of shipping from the captive countries which has taken refuge here or in the harbours of the Empire. Our stocks of food of all kinds are far more abundant than in the days of peace and a large and growing programme of food production is on foot.

Why do I say all this? Not assuredly to boast; not assuredly to give the slightest countenance to complacency. The dangers we face are still enormous, but so are our advantages and resources. I recount them because the people have a right to know that there are solid grounds for the confidence which we feel, and that we have good reason to believe ourselves capable, as I said in a very dark hour two months ago, of continuing the war " if necessary alone, if necessary for years." I say it also because the fact that the British Empire stands invincible, and that Nazidom is still being resisted, will kindle again the spark of hope in the breasts of hundreds of millions of down-trodden or despairing men and women throughout Europe, and far beyond its bounds, and that from these sparks there will presently come a cleansing and devouring flame.

The great air battle which has been in progress over this Island for the last few weeks has recently attained a high intensity. It is too soon to attempt to assign limits either to its scale or to its duration. We must certainly expect that greater efforts will be made by the enemy than any he has so far put forth. Hostile air fields are still being developed in France and the Low Countries, and the movement of squadrons and material for attacking us is still proceeding. It is quite plain that Herr Hitler could not admit defeat in his air attack on Great Britain without sustaining most serious injury. If, after all his boastings and blood-curdling threats and lurid accounts trumpeted round the world of the damage he has inflicted, of the vast numbers of our Air Force he has shot down, so he says, with so little loss to himself; if after tales of the panic-stricken British crouched in their holes cursing the plutocratic Parliament which has led them to such a plight; if after all this his whole air onslaught were forced after a while tamely to peter out, the Führer's reputation for veracity of statement might be seriously impugned. We may be sure, therefore, that he will continue as long

as he has the strength to do so, and as long as any preoccupations he may have in respect of the Russian Air Force allow him to do so.

On the other hand, the conditions and course of the fighting have so far been favourable to us. I told the House two months ago that whereas in France our fighter aircraft were wont to inflict a loss of two or three to one upon the Germans, and in the fighting at Dunkirk, which was a kind of no man's land, a loss of about three or four to one, we expected that in an attack on this Island we should achieve a larger ratio. This has certainly come true. It must also be remembered that all the enemy machines and pilots which are shot down over our Island, or over the seas which surround it, are either destroyed or captured; whereas a considerable proportion of our machines, and also of our pilots, are saved, and soon again in many cases come into action.

A vast and admirable system of salvage, directed by the Ministry of Aircraft Production, ensures the speediest return to the fighting line of damaged machines, and the most provident and speedy use of all the spare parts and material. At the same time the splendid, nay, astounding increase in the output and repair of British aircraft and engines which Lord Beaverbrook has achieved by a genius of organisation and drive, which looks like magic, has given us overflowing reserves of every type of aircraft, and an ever mounting stream of production both in quantity and quality. The enemy is, of course, far more numerous than we are. But our new production already, as I am advised, largely exceeds his, and the American production is only just beginning to flow in. It is a fact, as I see from my daily returns, that our bomber and fighter strengths now, after all this fighting, are larger than they have ever been. We hope, we believe that we shall be able to continue the air struggle indefinitely and as long as the enemy pleases, and the longer it continues the more rapid will be our approach, first towards that parity, and then into that superiority in the air, upon which in a large measure the decision of the war depends.

The gratitude of every home in our Island, in our Empire, and indeed throughout the world, except in the abodes of the guilty, goes out to the

[The Prime Minister.]

British airmen who, undaunted by odds, unwearied in their constant challenge and mortal danger, are turning the tide of world war by their prowess and by their devotion. Never in the field of human conflict was so much owed by so many to so few. All hearts go out to the fighter pilots, whose brilliant actions we see with our own eyes day after day, but we must never forget that all the time, night after night, month after month, our bomber squadrons travel far into Germany, find their targets in the darkness by the highest navigational skill, aim their attacks, often under the heaviest fire, often with serious loss, with deliberate, careful discrimination, and inflict shattering blows upon the whole of the technical and war-making structure of the Nazi power. On no part of the Royal Air Force does the weight of the war fall more heavily than on the daylight bombers who will play an invaluable part in the case of invasion and whose unflinching zeal it has been necessary in the meanwhile on numerous occasions to restrain.

We are able to verify the results of bombing military targets in Germany, not only by reports which reach us through many sources, but also, of course, by photography. I have no hesitation in saying that this process of bombing the military industries and communications of Germany and the air bases and storage depots from which we are attacked, which process will continue upon an ever-increasing scale until the end of the war, and may in another year attain dimensions hitherto undreamed of, affords one at least of the most certain, if not the shortest of all the roads to victory. Even if the Nazi legions stood triumphant on the Black Sea, or indeed upon the Caspian, even if Hitler was at the gates of India, it would profit him nothing if at the same time the entire economic and scientific apparatus of German war power lay shattered and pulverised at home.

The fact that the invasion of this Island upon a large scale has become a far more difficult operation with every week that has passed since we saved our Army at Dunkirk, and our very great preponderance of sea power, enable us to turn our eyes and to turn our strength increasingly towards the Mediterranean and against that other enemy who, without the slightest provocation, coldly and deliberately, for greed and gain, stabbed France in the back in the moment of her agony, and is now marching against us in Africa. The defection of France has, of course, been deeply damaging to our position in what is called, somewhat oddly, the Middle East. In the defence of Somaliland, for instance, we had counted upon strong French forces attacking the Italians from Jibuti. We had counted also upon the use of the French naval and air bases in the Mediterranean, and particularly upon the North African shore. We had counted upon the French Fleet. Even though metropolitan France was temporarily overrun, there was no reason why the French Navy, substantial parts of the French Army, the French Air Force and the French Empire overseas should not have continued the struggle at our side.

Shielded by overwhelming sea-power, possessed of invaluable strategic bases and of ample funds, France might have remained one of the great combatants in the struggle. By so doing, France would have preserved the continuity of her life, and the French Empire might have advanced with the British Empire to the rescue of the independence and integrity of the French Motherland. In our own case, if we had been put in the terrible position of France, a contingency now happily impossible, although, of course, it would have been the duty of all war leaders to fight on here to the end, it would also have been their duty, as I indicated in my speech of 4th June, to provide as far as possible for the Naval security of Canada and our Dominions and to make sure they had the means to carry on the struggle from beyond the oceans. Most of the other countries that have been overrun by Germany for the time being have persevered valiantly and faithfully. The Czechs, the Poles, the Norwegians, the Dutch, the Belgians are still in the field, sword in hand, recognised by Great Britain and the United States as the sole representative authorities and lawful Governments of their respective States.

That France alone should lie prostrate at this moment, is the crime, not of a great and noble nation, but of what are called " the men of Vichy." We have profound sympathy with the French people. Our old comradeship with France is not dead. In General de Gaulle and his gallant band, that comradeship takes an effective form. These free Frenchmen have been condemned to death by Vichy, but the day will come, as surely as the sun will rise to-morrow, when their names will be held in honour, and their names will be graven in stone in the streets and villages of a France restored in a liberated Europe to its full freedom and its ancient fame. But this conviction which I feel of the future cannot affect the immediate problems which confront us in the Mediterranean and in Africa. It had been decided some time before the beginning of the war not to defend the Protectorate of Somaliland, and when our small forces there, a few battalions, a few guns, were attacked by all the Italian troops, nearly two divisions, which had formerly faced the French at Jibuti, it was right to withdraw our detachments, virtually intact, for action elsewhere. Far larger operations no doubt impend in the Middle East theatre, and I shall certainly not attempt to discuss or prophesy about their probable course. We have large armies and many means of reinforcing them. We have the complete sea command of the Eastern Mediterranean. We intend to do our best to give a good account of ourselves, and to discharge faithfully and resolutely all our obligations and duties in that quarter of the world. More than that I do not think the House would wish me to say at the present time.

A good many people have written to me to ask me to make on this occasion a fuller statement of our war aims, and of the kind of peace we wish to make after the war, than is contained in the very considerable declaration which was made early in the Autumn. Since then we have made common cause with Norway, Holland and Belgium. We have recognised the Czech Government of Dr. Benes, and we have told General de Gaulle that our success will carry with it the restoration of France. I do not think it would be wise at this moment, while the battle rages and the war is still perhaps only in its earlier stage, to embark upon elaborate speculations about the future shape which should be given to Europe or the new securities which must be arranged to spare mankind the miseries of a third World War. The ground is not new, it has been frequently traversed and explored, and many ideas are held about it in common by all good men,

and all free men. But before we can undertake the task of rebuilding we have not only to be convinced ourselves, but we have to convince all other countries that the Nazi tyranny is going to be finally broken. The right to guide the course of world history is the noblest prize of victory. We are still toiling up the hill, we have not yet reached the crest-line of it, we cannot survey the landscape or even imagine what its condition will be when that longed-for morning comes. The task which lies before us immediately is at once more practical, more simple and more stern. I hope—indeed I pray—that we shall not be found unworthy of our victory if after toil and tribulation it is granted to us. For the rest, we have to gain the victory. That is our task.

There is, however, one direction in which we can see a little more clearly ahead. We have to think not only for ourselves but for the lasting security of the cause and principles for which we are fighting and of the long future of the British Commonwealth of Nations. Some months ago we came to the conclusion that the interests of the United States and of the British Empire both required that the United States should have facilities for the naval and air defence of the Western hemisphere against the attack of a Nazi power which might have acquired temporary but lengthy control of a large part of Western Europe and its formidable resources. We had therefore decided spontaneously, and without being asked or offered any inducement, to inform the Government of the United States that we would be glad to place such defence facilities at their disposal by leasing suitable sites in our Transatlantic possessions for their greater security against the unmeasured dangers of the future. The principle of association of interests for common purposes between Great Britain and the United States had developed even before the war. Various agreements had been reached about certain small islands in the Pacific Ocean which had become important as air fuelling points. In all this line of thought we found ourselves in very close harmony with the Government of Canada.

Presently we learned that anxiety was also felt in the United States about the air and naval defence of their Atlantic seaboard, and President Roosevelt has recently made it clear that he would like

[The Prime Minister.]

to discuss with us, and with the Dominion of Canada and with Newfoundland, the development of American naval and air facilities in Newfoundland and in the West Indies. There is, of course, no question of any transference of sovereignty —that has never been suggested—or of any action being taken, without the consent or against the wishes of the various Colonies concerned, but for our part, His Majesty's Government are entirely willing to accord defence facilities to the United States on a 99 years' leasehold basis, and we feel sure that our interests no less than theirs, and the interests of the Colonies themselves and of Canada and Newfoundland will be served thereby. These are important steps. Undoubtedly this process means that these two great organisations of the English-speaking democracies, the British Empire and the United States, will have to be somewhat mixed up together in some of their affairs for mutual and general advantage. For my own part, looking out upon the future, I do not view the process with any misgivings. I could not stop it if I wished; no one can stop it. Like the Mississippi, it just keeps rolling along. Let it roll. Let it roll on full flood, inexorable, irresistible, benignant, to broader lands and better days.

Jan. 20
1941

THE WHITE HOUSE
WASHINGTON

Dear Churchill

Wendell Willkie will give you
this — He is truly helping to keep
politics out over here.

I think this verse applies to your
people as it does to us:

"Sail on, Oh Ship of State!
Sail on Oh Union strong and great.
Humanity with all its fears,
With all the hopes of future years
Is hanging breathless on thy fate"

As ever yours

Franklin D Roosevelt

August the 14th 1941

CHURCHILL (MRS)
P. & P.

5

10, Downing Street,
Whitehall,

CSC
TRUST

Champneys
Tring

My Darling This morning Early
my Wireless told me that
at 3 o'clock Mr Attlee
would be making a statement
on behalf of the Government
& that simultaneously the
same announcement would be
given out from the White
House in Washington. Great
excitement & anticipation —
It cannot be a declaration

of War by America ... Because
the President cannot do that
without Congress ?

I am told that in
this Retreat (which I leave this
afternoon), the Patients have
been betting whether I am
have gone to see the Presi-
-dent or Stalin . I will
conclude my letter after
hearing the broadcast . So
back to Chequers this af-
-ternoon & a dispatch
rider is coming to fetch
this letter for the pouch .
I am longing to

CSC TRUST

10, Downing Street,
Whitehall.

Dear One

see you my
I pray. Our journey has
been fruitful & that you
& the President like
each other. This place has
done me a great deal
of good. I feel rested &
refreshed. "Wow & Re Wow"
Tomorrow Mary & I are
going to Bailiffscourt to
spend the week. End with

- Walter Moyne. And when
return to London. Monday perhaps
you may be nearly home.
Last Sunday I inspected
a very smart platoon of Home
Guard of which the Director
of this place is commanding
Officer – They work very hard
doing all sorts of exercises
creeping about the woods
at night & taking the local
villages at the point of the
bayonet. 3.20. I have
just heard your joint declaration.
It is grand. God bless you
Clemmie

(THIS DOCUMENT IS THE PROPERTY OF HIS BRITANNIC MAJESTY'S GOVERNMENT).

TO BE KEPT UNDER LOCK AND KEY.

S E C R E T.　　It is requested that special care may be taken to　COPY NO. *88*
　　　　　　　　ensure the secrecy of this document.

CABINET WAR ROOM RECORD NO. 827.

For the 24 Hours ending 0700, 8th December, 1941.

NAVAL.

CHINA.

1.　　At 2143 yesterday orders were given to commence
hostilities against Japan, it having been reported that at
1846 an attempt was being made by the Japanese to land troops
at KOTA BAHRU (north east MALAYA) and that PEARL Harbour,
HONOLULU had been attacked by Japanese aircraft and U-Boats.
In this attack U.S. Battleship OKLAHOMA capsized, a destroyer
in dock was blown up and U.S. Battleship TENNESSEE, a destroyer
and a minelayer were set on fire.
　　　　Four airfields were attacked and hangars and some
planes on the ground were set on fire.　The power stations were
also hit but not put out of action.
　　　　Heavy casualties to personnel are reported.　One
U-Boat and at least two enemy aircraft were destroyed.
　　　　At 2130, 18 aircraft attacked SINGAPORE but no naval
damage was done.

MEDITERRANEAN.

2.　　Yesterday afternoon H.M. Sloop FLAMINGO was seriously
damaged by bombs and H.M. Armed Boarding vessel CHANTALA was
mined in TOBRUK harbour.

3.　　On the 1st December H.M. Submarine REGENT sank the
Italian s.s. ERICE (2,353) northbound, about 65 miles north
of PANTELLARIA.

WEST ATLANTIC.

4.　　H.M. Canadian Corvette WINDFLOWER was sunk in collision
150 miles west of CAPE RACE.

ENEMY ATTACK ON TRADE.

5.　　s.s. WELSH PRINCE (5,148) in northbound coastal
convoy was mined off the WASH yesterday afternoon.

MILITARY.

LIBYA.

6.　　On 6th December, the 15th German Armoured Division,
supported by infantry, moved against BIR EL GOBI from the
north west, whilst the 21st German Armoured Division, with
remnants of the Italian Ariete Division, remained just east of
EL ADEM.　Towards evening the enemy mounted an attack on one
of our formations west of BIR EL GOBI but it did not develop.

On morning 7th December, enemy tanks, probably comprising both 15th and 21st Armoured Divisions, were still reported west of BIR EL GOBI and were being engaged by our armoured and unarmoured troops.

Yesterday, patrols from TOBRUK joined hands at SIDI REZEGH with armoured car patrols which had advanced from the south. 18 abandoned German tanks and much material including wireless equipment were found in this area.

FAR EAST.

7.   In the Japanese attack on KOTA BHARU it appears that the first attack was repulsed, but subsequently enemy troops succeeded in landing and are reported infiltrating towards KOTA BHARU aerodrome. They are being engaged by our land and air forces.

RUSSIA.

8.   Moscow Sector. German pressure is being maintained towards MOSCOW from the north, and in the TULA area where further slight German gains are reported. The Russians however continued to deliver counter-attacks.

Rostov Sector.   There is no information that the Germans have been forced westwards from their line on the River MIUS.

AIR.

R.A.F. OPERATIONS.

9.   Yesterday, a 800 ton merchant vessel off the Dutch coast was attacked by a Hudson and was left sinking. In the course of offensive operations over Northern France fighters attacked the DIEPPE Power Station.   One Spitfire is missing.

Last Night.   254 aircraft were despatched as follows:- AACHEN 132, BREST 31, CALAIS 24, OSTEND 23, DUNKIRK 22, BOULOGNE 19 Leaflets (HOLLAND, PARIS, ORLEANS) 3. Three aircraft are missing, and one crashed on return. Landing reports have not yet been received from 122 which went out late.

LIBYA.   On the 6th December two squadrons of Marylands and four squadrons of Blenheims attacked M.T. in the EL ADEM area. Bombs fell among groups of tanks, tank-carriers and M.T. Beaufighters attacked M.T. on the DERNA - TOBRUK road, and aircraft on the ground at EL TMIMI, five of which were damaged. Hurricanes machine-gunned JEDABYA landing ground destroying four enemy aircraft and damaging seven. On the night 6th/7th Wellingtons made two heavy attacks on stationary M.T. on the EL ADEM - ACROMA - EL GAZALA road, causing many petrol fires.

TRIPOLI (L). On the 6th Blenheims from MALTA scored hits on barracks at HOMS, and on the following night naval aircraft bombed the aerodrome at CASTEL BENITO.

ITALY.   On the night 6th/7th Wellingtons attacked the Royal Arsenal at NAPLES dropping 13 tons of bombs in a raid which lasted $5\frac{1}{2}$ hours. Fires were started in the target area, in the docks and in railway centres.

ENEMY ACTIVITY.

10.   Last Night. 41 aircraft operated against this country. Five of these made landfall.

HOME SECURITY.

11.   About 100 incendiary bombs were dropped at GRIMSBY at about 1850, causing some small fires in the fish docks and in dwelling houses, and nine minor casualties. There have been no other incidents to report.

INTELLIGENCE.

JAPANESE AIRCRAFT IN INDO-CHINA.

12.   The total number of Japanese aircraft in French Indo-China is now about 350, disposed approximately, 100 in the North and 250 in the South. The total number of fighters probably does not exceed 100.

REFLEX 177
TOO 2105Z/21
TOR 1050A/22

IMMEDIATE

MOST SECRET CYPHER TELEGRAM

From:-   Mideast

To:-   Air Ministry

_____

REFLEX 177   21.8.42.

        Following Most Secret and Personal from Prime
Minister to Deputy Prime Minister for War Cabinet, General
Ismay and others concerned.

1.   Have just spent two days in the Western Desert
visiting H.Q. Eighth Army.   Brooke, Alexander, Montgomery
and I went round together seeing 44th Division 7th
Armoured and 22nd Armoured Brigade and representatives of
the New Zealand Division.   I saw a great number of men and all
the principal Commanders in the 13th Corps area, also again
Air Marshal Conyngham who shares headquarters with General
Montgomery.

2.   I am sure we were heading for disaster under the
former regime.   The Army was reduced to bits and pieces
and oppressed by a sense of bafflement and uncertainty.
Apparently it was intended in face of heavy attack to
retire eastwards to the Delta.   Many were looking over
their shoulders to make sure of their seat in the lorry
and no plain plan of battle or dominating will power
had reached the units.   It would only have needed the
arrival of General Corbett, a very small agreeable man,
of no personality and little experience, to take command
of the Eighth Army, as Auchinleck was on the verge of
ordering him to do for the last month, in order to have
produced a most grave situation.

3.   So serious did this appear that General Montgomery
insisted on taking command of the Eighth Army as soon as
he had visited the Front, and by Alexander's decision the
whole command in the Middle East was transferred on the
13th, not without displeasure to Auchinleck.

4.   Since then a complete change of atmosphere has
taken place from what I could see myself of the troops
and hear from their Commanders.   Alexander ordered
Montgomery to prepare to take the offensive and
meanwhile to hold all positions and Montgomery issued an
invigorating directive to his Commanders, of which I
will circulate the text on my return.   The highest alacrity
and activity prevails.   Positions are everywhere being

                                      strengthened ....

strengthened and extended forces are being sorted out and re-
grouped in solid units.   The 44th and the 10th Armoured
Division have already arrived in the forward zone.   The
roads are busy with the forward movement of troops, tanks
and guns.   General Horrocks commands the 13th Corps.
Ramsden (?) will be left for the present with the 30th Corps.
General Lumsden is forming the 10th Corps for mass of manoeu-
vre for the offensive battle towards the end of September.
For this a bold and comprehensive plan has been made.

5.   However, it seems probable that Rommel will
attack during the moon period before the end of August.
He has lost valuable shipments, on which he counted, and
under-rates our strength, but we must not under-rate his.
We must expect a very wide turning movement by perhaps
20,000 Germans and 15,000 Italians, comprising formations
of two Panzer and 4 or 5 Axis motorized divisions.   The
ensuing battle will be hard and critical but I have the
greatest confidence in Alexander and Montgomery, and I
feel sure the Army will fight as it has not fought since the
beginning of the Gazala battle.   If Rommel does not attack
in August he will be attacked himself at greater relative
disadvantage in September.   This would fit in well with
TORCH.

6.   For an August battle we should have at the front
about 700 tanks, with 100 replacements, about 700 service-
able aircraft, 500 field guns, nearly 400 6-pdr and 440
2-pdr A/A guns, but as we have only 24 medium guns we are
definitely weaker in medium artillery.   As parachute descents
must be expected on a large scale and Rommel will no doubt
bid high for victory, the Army will be extended to the full.

7.   To give the fullest manoeuvring power to the Eighth
Army in the event of it being attacked next week, a strong
line of defence is being developed along the Delta from
Alexandria to Cairo.   The 51st Division is taking station
there.   I shall visit it to-morrow.   I drew General
Alexander's attention to the inundation (?) plans which
we made two years ago and action has been taken at various
points.

8.   To sum up, while I and others would prefer the
September to the August battle because of the greater
certainty, our army will eagerly meet the enemy should he
attack, and I am satisfied that we have lively, confident
resolute men in command working together as an admirable
team under a leader of the highest military quality.
Everything has been done and is being done that is possible,
and it is now my duty to return home as I have no part
to play in the battle which must now be left to those in
whom we place our trust.   I have still a good deal of
business to settle.   As you will see from other telegrams
Gort is here and Platt arrives tomorrow.   C.I.G.S and
I plan to start Sunday night by a route which you will

learn.....

THE CHARTWELL TRUST

26

learn in a separate telegram.   I hope to be available
for my weekly luncheon with the King on Tuesday if
that should be His Majesty's wish.

9.   My general impression of Jubilee is that the
results fully justified the heavy cost.   The large
scale air battle alone justified the raid.

10.   I thank you all most warmly for the support you
have given me while engaged in these anxious and none
too-pleasant tasks.

T.O.O. 2105Z/21

(Circulation)
War Cabinet Offices.

THE
CHARTWELL
TRUST

A.M. FORM No. 1479 TOP ~~MOST~~ SECRET ULTRA

TO BE KEPT UNDER LOCK AND KEY AND NEVER TO BE REMOVED FROM THE OFFICE.
THIS FORM IS TO BE USED FOR AIR INTELLIGENCE MESSAGES ONLY.

NR. No.	GR. No.		OFFICE SERIAL No.
DATE	TIME OF RECEIPT	TIME OF DESPATCH	SYSTEM
TO :			
FROM :			
SENDERS No.			

(T.O.O. VARIOUS 6/6/44).

CX/MSS/T207/57

(ZTPG/248973, 248970, 248974,
278977, 248981, 248980).

KV/6634.

W E S T   E U R O P E.

COMPILED FROM DOCUMENT DATED 6/6, SEEN BY SOURCE :-

TIME OF
DESPATCH

"SDC NORMANDY ON 6TH

(A) ~~1000~~ *10 am* HOURS.   SITUATION AT ASNELLES.   FURTHER

DISEMBARKATIONS BETWEEN ABOUT 1 KILOMETRE AND

10 KILOMETRES TO EASTWARD.   TANKS AND INFANTRY (STRONG

INDICATIONS OPERATING) AGAINST ASNELLES.   ARROMANCHES

UNDER FIRE.   REINFORCED AIR RECCE.   LONGUES STILL UNDER

FIRE.

(B) ~~1030~~ *10.30 am* HOURS RADAR STATION ARROMANCHES UNDER FIRE FROM

SHIPS' GUNS AND (STRONG INDICATIONS SURROUNDED) BY TANKS

AND INFANTRY.

(C) ~~1100~~ *11 am* HOURS CONTINUOUS ARRIVALS AND DEPARTURES FROM

DISTRIBUTION :			
DEGREE OF PRIORITY	TIME OF ORIGIN	SIGNATURE OF ORIGINATOR, NOT TO BE TELEPRINTED	OPERATOR'S RECEIPT

A.M. FORM No. 1479 TOP ~~MOST~~ SECRET ULTRA

TO BE KEPT UNDER LOCK AND KEY AND NEVER TO BE REMOVED FROM THE OFFICE.
THIS FORM IS TO BE USED FOR AIR INTELLIGENCE MESSAGES ONLY.

NR. No.	GR. No.		OFFICE SERIAL No.
DATE	TIME OF RECEIPT	TIME OF DESPATCH	SYSTEM

TO:

FROM:

PAGE TWO.

SENDERS No.

CX/MSS/T207/57 (CONT'D).

VIRE ESTUARY.   SLIGHT ARTILLERY ACTIVITY.

(D) ~~1200~~ *Noon* HOURS LEFT-HAND MARCOUF ISLAND OCCUPIED BY

ALLIES AND AT ~~1210~~ *12.10pm* HOURS HEAVY BOMBING ATTACK ON

GATTEVILLE BATTERY, NO FURTHER DETAILS KNOWN.

(E) ~~1500~~ *3pm* HOURS: FAIRLY LARGE SHIPPING FORMATIONS,

ALSO LANDING CRAFT, STATIONARY, NORTHEAST TO EAST OF

BARFLEUR, 40 TO 50 KILOMETRES DISTANT.

SECONDLY.   ADMIRAL CHANNEL COAST REPORTED AT ~~1345~~ *1.15pm* HRS.

6TH. SEINE-SOMME SECTOR: NORTH OF SEINE QUIET SO FAR.

SOUTH OF SEINE CLEARED OF AIR LANDING TROOPS.   NO LANDINGS

FROM SEA.   PAS DE CALAIS SECTOR: NOTHING TO REPORT".

KV/6634/SH/AG/FU/ON/EF/TA/XF IS BEING PASSED AT ~~1855Z~~ *6.55pm.* /6/6/44.

BB/AM/WO/ADY   RFB/AB/KD   2005/6/6/44Z.

RD HM.

DISTRIBUTION:

DEGREE OF PRIORITY	TIME OF ORIGIN	SIGNATURE OF ORIGINATOR. NOT TO BE TELEPRINTED	OPERATOR'S RECEIPT

THIS DOCUMENT IS THE PROPERTY OF HIS BRITANNIC MAJESTY'S GOVERNMENT

Printed for the War Cabinet. July 1944.

SECRET.

Copy No.

52

W.M. (44)

95th Conclusions.

WAR CABINET 95 (44).

CONCLUSIONS of a Meeting of the War Cabinet held in the Cabinet War Room, S.W. 1, on Monday, 24th July, 1944, at 6 p.m.

Present :

The Right Hon. WINSTON S. CHURCHILL, M.P., Prime Minister (*in the Chair*).

The Right Hon. C. R. ATTLEE, M.P., Lord President of the Council.

The Right Hon. ANTHONY EDEN, M.P., Secretary of State for Foreign Affairs.

The Right Hon. Sir JOHN ANDERSON, M.P., Chancellor of the Exchequer.

The Right Hon. ERNEST BEVIN, M.P., Minister of Labour and National Service.

The Right Hon. OLIVER LYTTELTON, M.P., Minister of Production.

The Right Hon. HERBERT MORRISON, M.P., Secretary of State for the Home Department and Minister of Home Security.

The Right Hon. LORD WOOLTON, Minister of Reconstruction.

The following were also present :

The Hon. Sir FIROZ KHAN NOON, Representative of the Government of India.

The Right Hon. VISCOUNT CRANBORNE, Secretary of State for Dominion Affairs.

The Right Hon. L. S. AMERY, M.P., Secretary of State for India and Secretary of State for Burma.

The Right Hon. A. V. ALEXANDER, M.P., First Lord of the Admiralty.

The Right Hon. Sir JAMES GRIGG, M.P., Secretary of State for War.

The Right Hon. SIR ARCHIBALD SINCLAIR, Bt., M.P., Secretary of State for Air.

The Right Hon. Sir STAFFORD CRIPPS, K.C., M.P., Minister of Aircraft Production.

The Right Hon. H. U. WILLINK, K.C., M.P., Minister of Health (*Item 5*).

The Right Hon. LORD LEATHERS, Minister of War Transport (*Item 5*).

The Right Hon. LORD PORTAL, Minister of Works (*Item 5*).

The Right Hon. BRENDAN BRACKEN, M.P., Minister of Information.

The Right Hon. LORD CHERWELL, Paymaster-General.

Mr. DUNCAN SANDYS, M.P., Joint Parliamentary Secretary, Ministry of Supply (*Item 5*).

The Hon. Sir ALEXANDER CADOGAN, Permanent Under-Secretary of State for Foreign Affairs (*Items 1–3*).

Admiral of the Fleet Sir ANDREW CUNNINGHAM, First Sea Lord and Chief of Naval Staff.

Marshal of the Royal Air Force Sir CHARLES F. A. PORTAL, Chief of the Air Staff.

Field-Marshal Sir ALAN BROOKE, Chief of the Imperial General Staff.

Secretariat.

Sir EDWARD BRIDGES.
General Sir HASTINGS L. ISMAY.
Sir GILBERT LAITHWAITE.
Mr. W. S. MURRIE.
Mr. L. F. BURGIS.

[27949—1]

B

WAR CABINET 95 (44).

Contents.

Naval, Military and Air Operations.

(Previous Reference: W.M.(44)91st Conclusions, Minute 1.)

Air Operations.

Home Theatre.

1. The Chiefs of Staff reported the principal events of the previous week.

Bad weather had again interfered with bombing operations, but our bombers had flown 5,500 sorties and dropped 18,000 tons of bombs, a third of which had been on Germany. 5,000 tons had been dropped in the preliminary bombardment before the Allied attack south of Caen.

Bomber Command had also attacked synthetic oil plants in the Ruhr and " Crossbow " targets. Mosquitoes had attacked Berlin.

United States heavy bombers had flown 6,200 sorties and dropped 12,400 tons of bombs, 8,700 tons of them on targets in Germany, which had included experimental stations at Peenemunde and Zinnowitz, aircraft factories and oil installations.

British and American heavy bombers had had a record week, dropping in all 30,500 tons of bombs.

The Allied Expeditionary Air Force had flown 7,500 sorties.

The enemy had lost 192 aircraft against Allied losses of 283.

Flying-Bombs.

During the week 802 flying-bombs had been launched, of which 349, or 43 per cent., had been destroyed and 263 had reached London. The fighters had accounted for 60 per cent., A.A. guns for 30 per cent. and the Balloons for 10 per cent. of those destroyed.

Mediterranean.

In the Mediterranean, Allied aircraft had dropped 8,500 tons of bombs, mainly on oil plants, aircraft factories and other targets in South-East Europe.

Naval Operations.

During the previous week there had been no shipping losses due to enemy action. Total losses for July to date, including belated reports, amounted to 51,273 tons.

Six U-boats had been destroyed so far this month.

U-boat Warfare.

The Prime Minister said that, at the request of the Admiralty, he had suggested to President Roosevelt that, before the next monthly statement* on U-boat warfare was published, an interim statement should be made emphasising the notable achievement of our small craft and aircraft in holding off attacks by U-boats against shipping engaged in the " Overlord " operation. The President had replied deprecating this suggestion, mainly, he thought, on security grounds.

The Prime Minister asked the First Lord of the Admiralty to send him the material which the Admiralty wished to publish on this matter, and said that he would then consider making a further approach to the President.

Clearance of Mines in Cherbourg Harbour.

Reference was also made to the clearance of mines in Cherbourg Harbour, which had been done by British divers. This feat deserved public acknowledgment.

The Prime Minister said that, provided security reasons permitted, he would consider including some reference to this matter in his forthcoming speech to Parliament on the war situation.

Military Operations. Normandy.

The Chief of the Imperial General Staff described the attack made by the Second British Army on the 18th July southwards from Caen. Some delay in getting our forces across the river, together with the fact that the Germans had been very quick in organising an anti-tank screen, had limited the success of this operation. West of St. Lo the United States forces had made some progress. Bad weather was hampering operations on the whole front.

The Prime Minister said that during his visit to Normandy he had visited a great number of troops and never had he seen an army which looked so well or so happy. General Montgomery had expressed his great satisfaction with the equipment and supplies with which, thanks to our military authorities, the army had been supplied.

Italy.

In Italy we had advanced along the whole front and both Leghorn and Ancona had been captured.

* See W.M. (43) 96th Conclusions, Minute 1.

Russia.

The Russian offensive had made great progress during the previous week. That day the Germans had admitted their retirement from Siedlice and Jaroslaw. Russian forces were very close to Brest Litovsk. The German Armies in Estonia and Latvia still showed no signs of attempting to withdraw.

The War Cabinet—
Took note of these statements.

Prisoners of War.

2. *The Secretary of State for War* said that a Court of Enquiry had been held on the 7th July, 1944, to investigate the death at Audrieu, in Normandy, of certain Canadian and British officers. The Court had found as follows :—

(*a*) one Canadian officer, 23 other ranks and 2 British soldiers met their death at or near the Château d'Audrieu on or about the 8th June, 1944;

(*b*) the Canadian officer and 18 of the Canadian soldiers were prisoners of war in the custody of the German army;

(*c*) they had been murdered by members of the 12th S.S. Reconnaissance Battalion of the 12th S.S. Panzer Division (Hitler Jugend) under the direction of certain of their officers;

(*d*) five Canadian and 2 British soldiers were in all probability prisoners of war in the hands of the same unit and suffered a similar fate to the officer and 18 soldiers.

This report had been forwarded to the Combined Chiefs of Staff, and up to date no information had been received as to what action was being taken by them. A copy of the report had also been furnished to the Canadian Military Headquarters in London. It would be necessary to reach agreement with the Canadian Government as to what should be said on this matter.

The War Cabinet—
Took note of this statement.

Foreign Affairs.

Germany.

3. *The Secretary of State for Foreign Affairs* referred to the attempt which had been made on Hitler's life. Authentic information was very difficult to come by, but there seemed little doubt that there had been, and perhaps still was, a movement of considerable force in Germany behind the Generals. It was still impossible to judge what the consequences would be, but, if the German Government were successful in repressing the movement, the result for the time being would be to rivet the Nazi machine still more firmly on the German nation.

A discussion followed as to what line the Secretary of State for Foreign Affairs should take in the matter in the House of Commons on the following day. The general sense of the War Cabinet was that at this stage the less said the better. Thus it might be stated that as to a great deal of the affair everyone could judge for himself, but that His Majesty's Government had not yet reached a point in the assessment of the evidence at which a public statement on their behalf would be appropriate.

Poland.
(Previous Reference :
W.M.(44)47th Conclusions,
Minute 2.)

The Secretary of State for Foreign Affairs reported to the War Cabinet the latest developments in Russo-Polish relations. A record of the discussion and the conclusions reached is contained in the Secretary's Standard File of War Cabinet Conclusions.

Air Raids.
(Previous
Reference:
W.M.(44)91st
Conclusions,
Minute 7.)
Attacks by
Flying-Bombs.

4. *The Home Secretary and Minister of Home Security* stated that up to 6 a.m. that morning the total casualties from flying-bombs reported were 4,089 killed, 12,126 seriously injured, 14,460 slightly injured and 46 unclassified, making a grand total of 30,721. Arrangements in the reception areas under the evacuation scheme were going better. He would be able to give an encouraging report at the confidential meeting with Members of Parliament fixed for the following day.

Air Raids.
(Previous
Reference:
W.M.(44)89th
Conclusions,
Minute 8.)

Attacks by
Flying-Bombs.

5. At their Meeting on the 10th July (W.M. (44) 89th Conclusions, Minute 8) the War Cabinet had invited the Home Secretary and Minister of Home Security to bring before the Civil Defence Committee the question of improving the public warning system, with particular reference to the possibility of an extension of the system of giving warning of imminent danger.

The War Cabinet now had before them a Memorandum by the Home Secretary and Minister of Home Security (W.P. (44) 401) reporting the result of the consideration given to the matter by the Civil Defence Committee.

Public Warning
System.

The Home Secretary and Minister of Home Security pointed out that, as experience was gained by flying-bomb attacks, the period of the alert was becoming more and more closely adjusted to the period of actual danger. There was, however, a considerable demand for some sort of imminent danger warning within the alert. The Civil Defence Committee had been unable to reach agreement on whether a system of imminent danger warning should or should not be instituted, but their view was that, if any system were to be adopted, it should consist of the display of a red storm cone on premises connected to the industrial alarm system, supplemented by a bell signal audible to the public in the neighbourhood of the premises. It would be impossible to cover the whole of London by a system of this kind, nor would it be infallible in its operation; and this would have to be made clear by the Government should it be decided to adopt the system. Whatever decision was taken, it seemed very desirable to standardise the unofficial and unco-ordinated system of warnings on private premises which had grown up since the flying-bomb attacks began.

It was generally agreed in discussion that any system of imminent danger warnings should be based on the industrial alarm scheme, which had reached a very high state of efficiency. It was felt, however, that a visible signal was open to considerable objection, particularly from the point of view of road traffic, and that a system under which localised signals would be given by the ringing of bells or the sounding of klaxons would be preferable.

The following additional points were raised in discussion :—

(*a*) *The Minister of Aircraft Production* stressed the fact that workers who received imminent danger warnings in factories were dissatisfied because their families did not receive the same warnings.

(*b*) *The Minister of War Transport* said that bus drivers were in favour of a system of imminent danger warnings within the alert.

(*c*) *The Minister of Production* pointed out that the production of the necessary equipment for the proposed system of audible warnings might present some difficulties.

The War Cabinet—

(1) Agreed that it was desirable to institute a system of localised audible warnings of imminent danger within the alert, based on the existing industrial alarm scheme.

(2) Invited the Home Secretary and Minister of Home Security, the Minister of Aircraft Production, the Minister of War Transport and the Minister of Works to settle

urgently by what means such a system could be most effectively and quickly provided. The assistance of other Ministers should be called on, as required, and a report of the conclusions reached should be submitted to the Prime Minister.

(3) Agreed that any announcement regarding the system should make it clear that it would be neither universal nor wholly effective.

Select Committee on National Expenditure.

Report on Tank Production. (Previous Reference: W.M.(44)68th Conclusions, Minute 4.)

6. On the 24th May the War Cabinet had before them a Memorandum (W.P. (44) 262) about the Report from the Select Committee on National Expenditure on Tank Production, and had decided that an interim reply should be sent to Sir John Wardlaw-Milne.

The War Cabinet now had before them a Memorandum (W.P. (44) 400) containing—

(i) A draft letter for the Prime Minister to send to Sir John Wardlaw-Milne.
(ii) A draft reply to the Select Committee's Report prepared by the Minister of Production, the Secretary of State for War and the Minister of Supply as an enclosure to (i).
(iii) A summary of the reports received on the performance of British tanks.

The War Cabinet—

Expressed general agreement with these documents and invited the Prime Minister to despatch the letter and the enclosure to Sir John Wardlaw-Milne, subject to such modifications as might be settled in consultation with the Ministers concerned.*

Offices of the War Cabinet, S.W. 1,
       24th July, 1944.

* NOTE.—The letter and enclosure were despatched as drafted on the 2nd August, 1944.

10

PRIME MINISTER'S
<u>TOP SECRET.</u>
PERSONAL TELEGRAM

10, Downing Street,
Whitehall.

SERIAL No. D.83/5

Resubmitted see D.89/5

WITHDRAWN See Genl Ismay's minute a 20/4/45 submitting a redraft of this tg op

<u>GENERAL ISMAY FOR C.O.S. COMMITTEE.</u>
<u>C. A. S.</u>

It seems to me that the moment has come when the question of bombing of German cities simply for the sake of increasing the terror, though under other pretexts, should be reviewed.   Otherwise we shall come into control of an utterly ruined land.   We shall not, for instance, be able to get housing materials out of Germany for our own needs because some temporary provision would have to be made for the Germans themselves.   The destruction of Dresden remains a serious query against the conduct of Allied bombing.   I am of the opinion that military objectives must henceforward be more strictly studied in our own interests rather than that of the enemy.

The Foreign Secretary has spoken to me on this subject, and I feel the need for more precise concentration upon military objectives, such as oil and communications behind the immediate battle-zone, rather than on mere acts of terror and wanton destruction, however impressive.

28.3.45

PRIME MINISTER'S
PERSONAL TELEGRAM

10, Downing Street,
Whitehall.

SERIAL No. _T.374/5._

_T.366/5_

PRIME MINISTER TO GENERAL EISENHOWER.
   Personal and Top Secret.

Private & Confidential.

1.   Very many thanks for your Forward 18334.   It seems
to me personally that if the enemy's resistance does not
collapse, the shifting of the main axis of advance so much
farther to the southward and the withdrawal of the Ninth
U.S. Army from the 21st Army Group may stretch Montgomery's
front so widely that the offensive role which was assigned to
him may peter out.   I do not know whether it would be an
advantage not repeat not to cross the Elbe.   If the enemy's
resistance should weaken, as you evidently expect and which
may well be fulfilled, why should we not cross the Elbe and
advance as far eastward as possible?   This has an important
political bearing, as the Russian Armies of the South seem
certain to enter Vienna and overrun Austria.   If we
deliberately leave Berlin to them, even should it be in our
grasp, the double event may strengthen their conviction,
already apparent, that they have done everything.

2.   Further, I do not consider myself that Berlin has yet

lost its military and certainly not its political significance.
The fall of Berlin would have a profound psychological
effect on German resistance in every part of the Reich.
While Berlin holds out, great masses of Germans will feel it
their duty to go down fighting.   The idea that the capture
of Dresden and junction with the Russians there would be a
superior gain does not commend itself to me.   The parts of
the German Government Departments which have moved south can
very quickly
ᴸmove southward still.   But while Berlin remains under the

(handwritten: very quickly ... again)

German Flag, it cannot in my opinion fail to be the most
decisive point in Germany.

3.   Therefore I should greatly prefer persistence in the
plan on which we crossed the Rhine, namely that the Ninth
U.S. Army should march with the 21st Army Group to the Elbe
and beyond to Berlin.   This would not be in any way inconsis-
tent with the great central thrust which you are now so
rightly developing as the result of the brilliant operations
of your Armies south of the Ruhr.   It only shifts the weight
of one Army to the northern flank and thus avoids the
relegation of His Majesty's forces to an unexpectedly

restricted sphere.

4.   Of course I am treating this correspondence between

us as personal and private, just as if it was an unofficial

talk. ~~between us~~ I may use some q my arguments
     in other quarters
again, but not with reference to anything that has passed
between us.

                    WM

                31.3.45

10, Downing Street,
Whitehall.

Mr. Churchill has issued the following statement:-

"The decision of the British people has been
recorded in the votes counted to-day.   I have therefore
laid down the charge which was placed upon me in darker
times.   I regret that I have not been permitted to finish
the work against Japan.   For this however all plans and
preparations have been made, and the results may come much
quicker than we have hitherto been entitled to expect.
Immense responsibilities abroad and at home fall upon the
new Government, and we must all hope that they will be
successful in bearing them.

It only remains for me to express to the British
people, for whom I have acted in these perilous years, my
profound gratitude for the unflinching, unswerving support
which they have given me during my task, and for the many
expressions of kindness which they have shown towards their
servant."

26 . vii

CHURCHILL: THE WAR LEADER, 1940-1945

Churchill: The War Leader, 1940-1945 is the second in a new series of Document Packs on famous individuals. The first title, *Oscar Wilde: Trial and Punishment, 1895-1897* includes the famous calling card left by the Marquess of Queensberry that led directly to Wilde's downfall; a petition to Queen Victoria from Lord Alfred Douglas, pleading for Wilde's release from prison; and Oscar's poignant handwritten petition to the Home Secretary, describing his own fears of insanity.

> 'This is a cleverly designed, exciting publication . . . it allows the reader access to documents contemporaneous with the actual events of 1895-1897 and to encounter the players face to face . . . this material is neither embellished nor distorted; its interest lies in the compelling power of original statement.'
>
> *The Irish Times*

Please send us your comments on *Churchill: The War Leader, 1940-1945*:

	Very good	Good	Acceptable	Poor
Selection of documents	☐	☐	☐	☐
Quality of reproduction	☐	☐	☐	☐
Editorial text	☐	☐	☐	☐
Pack cover and design	☐	☐	☐	☐
Value for money	☐	☐	☐	☐

General comments for improvements to this pack and suggestions as to individuals we might cover in future packs would be welcome. If you are interested in any of the following titles, which are under consideration, please tick the appropriate boxes and return this form to the address below. Alternatively, complete the same form on our web site and e-mail your response: http://www.pro.gov.uk/bookshop/churchil.htm

Henry VIII and His Wives	☐ Trial and Execution of Charles I	☐
Mary Queen of Scots	☐ Oliver Cromwell	☐
Elizabeth I	☐ T E Lawrence	☐

If you wish to join the mailing list and be sent further information on PRO Document Packs and other titles, please return this form to Paul Sinnott, Sales and Marketing, Public Record Office, Ruskin Avenue, Kew, Richmond, Surrey, TW9 4DU, UK.

Name: . . . .

Address: . . . .

. . . .

. . . .

. . . .

Other PRO Document Packs

The *Battlefront* and *Official Story* series both focus on key events or campaigns, looking in detail at a particular day, event or battle from a number of different perspectives, drawing on contemporary case files, personal accounts, detailed reports, maps, plans, posters and photographs. Titles available in these series:

Battlefront: 1st July 1916. The First Day of the Somme   £12.99 inc VAT
  'A fascinating compilation'   John Keegan, Defence Editor, *Daily Telegraph*

Battlefront: 6th November 1917. The Fall of Passchendaele   £12.99 inc VAT
  'an admirable attempt to allow people to make up their own mind by examining the documents'   *Military Illustrated*

Titanic: 14th -15th April 1912. The Official Story   £14.99 inc VAT
  'A must for every *Titanic* enthusiast'   British Titanic Society

If you are interested in any of the following titles, which are under consideration, please tick the appropriate boxes:

Battle of Waterloo, 1815	☐
Charge of the Light Brigade, 1854	☐
Zulu War, 1879	☐
Boer War, 1899-1901	☐
Gallipoli, 1915	☐
German Spring Offensive, 1918	☐
Blitz, 1940	☐
Arnhem, 1944	☐
Lusitania: 7th May 1915. The Official Story	☐

Related World War Two titles

The Second World War. A Guide to Documents in the Public Record Office
J D Cantwell   revised edn, November 1998   £15.00

This guide details the vast amount of material relating to the Second World War held in the Public Record Office, in particular among the records of the Cabinet Office, the Foreign Office and the Armed Services. Last revised in 1993, this new edition is fully illustrated and incorporates material released since then, including Ultra decrypts, Special Operations Executive and MI5 records. No serious historian or enthusiast working on the Second World War can afford to be without this book.

The *PRO Publications Catalogue* is available from the address overleaf, or may be viewed on our web site: http://www.pro.gov.uk/bookshop/